DROWNING IN DEBT?

Get Out
And
Stay Out!

Alma Peterson

AJP BOOKS

Copyright © 1996 by Alma Peterson

All rights reserved under the Pan-American and International Copyright Conventions. Published in the United States by AJP BOOKS. This book may not be reproduced, in whole or in part, including photocopying, recording, or by any storage and retrieval system now known or hereafter invented, without written permission from the publisher.

Library of Congress Catalog Card Number: 96-96341

ISBN 0-9652507-0-9

Important Note: While the Author used the information in this book in order to achieve a debt-free lifestyle, each debt situation is different. The reader is encouraged to seek competent legal and financial advice regarding personal legal and financial decisions.

To order by mail send $9.50 plus $2.50 shipping and handling per copy to: AJP BOOKS, 825 College Blvd., Suite 102-303, Oceanside, CA 92057. Send questions and comments to the same address.

Printed in the United States 10 9 8 7 6 5 4 3 2

To my Mom, Mary Champion
and
to my Grandma, Ora Grantling.

Acknowledgments

I would like to thank my Husband Joseph for his patience, understanding and assistance during the writing of this book.

I would like to thank my cousin Sharon Kindell for her assistance.

I would also like to thank Nancy Kohler and Dolores Caponera for their assistance.

I want to express my humble gratitude for all the Lord Jesus has done in my life.

Contents

Preface   1
Introduction   3

First Step

Realizing you are in debt   7
  1. Deciding to make some changes   8
  2. What does being in debt mean to you?   9
  3. Fear of the unknown   10
  4. Not all debt is equal   12
  5. The stress of debt   13
  6. Who's to blame?   14
  7. Reaching out to others   15
  8. The attitude of avoidance   16
  9. Making efforts to contact creditors   17
 10. Friends and Family as creditors   20

Second Step

How did you get into debt?   21
  1. That first credit card   22
  2. That 2nd, 3rd, 4th, ... credit card   22
  3. Interest rates   23
  4. Credit card enticements   24
  5. The valued customer category   25
  6. Pre-approved credit applications   26
  7. Cash advances   26
  8. Haphazard spending   26
  9. Paying the minimum amount   28

Third Step

Exactly how much do you owe and what are your living expenses?   **31**
1. The total of all miscellaneous purchases   33
2. The total of all living expenses   35
3. The total of all credit cards and other debt   36
4. Create a simple filing system   37

Fourth Step

How much is your income?   **41**
1. How much are you paid each month?   42
2. A side note   43

Fifth Step

What is the difference between your expenses and what you make?   **47**
1. Making the commitment to move forward   48
2. What happens when you spend more than what you make? or How can you improve your monthly income?   49

Sixth Step

The process of getting out of Debt   **67**
1. Separating your monthly paychecks   68
2. Minimum amount due   71
3. Focusing on your lowest balance   71
4. Monthly "due dates"   73
5. Is that all I have left?   78
6. Pay-off projection dates   82
7. Don't get discouraged   87
8. Putting it all together   87

Seventh Step

Staying out of debt. **113**
  1. "Don't buy it if you can't pay for it" 114
  2. What about your new popularity? 118
  3. What's next? 119
  4. A final note 125

Preface

Several years ago, I fell into the trap of accepting every credit card that was offered to me by department stores, banks, and other credit card companies. I used these cards for everything. It wasn't very long until most of my income was being used to pay for long forgotten things I had purchased months and even years before. In addition to the credit cards, I had student loans, a car loan, and of course my daily living expenses. One day I sat down and figured out the total amount in loans and credit card bills I owed--the results were scary. Based on the way I was paying my bills, always the minimum amount due, it would have taken seventeen years to pay off what I had accumulated up to that date!

Even though I had just started a promising new career, my economic future did not look good at all. However, within three years of that date, and without taking out any additional loans, I was completely debt-free.

Not every one's debt situation is caused by the same circumstances and there are a number of remedies for getting out of debt. I will share with you, the system I developed and used to become debt-free. It took patience and dedication, but it worked for me.

Introduction

Consumer indebtedness now exceeds $1 trillion. One t r i l l i o n dollars! The concept of a "trillion" is foreign to most of us. But if you currently hold an account with any credit granting institution, with the exception of mortgages, you are included in this $1 trillion plus figure. The truth of the matter is most of us help compile this statistic in one form or another. What is startling about this figure is that as of 1994, more than $84 billion of the trillion dollar amount had been turned over to credit collection agencies. How did this happen? Was it the sluggish economy? Did people lose their jobs? Was there some unforeseen personal or family crisis? Or did millions of credit account holders miscalculate how much debt they could actually handle?

We all know the economy could be better and unemployment has been on the high side. And there are those family crises that will cause financial hardships. Clearly, all three of these factors can and do have some bearing on this startling statistic. Although these are contributing factors, are they the main reasons so many accounts are now in the hands of the collection police? No. The one factor that beats all others by a long shot is a lack of forethought by individual account holders.

Who wants to hear that? It would be better to blame the situation on the economy or on the depressed job market. But where is the solution to the problem when we shift the blame in those directions? There is no solution, instead we only get statistics. Webster's definition of statistics reads: facts or data of a numerical kind, assembled, classified, and tabulated so as to present significant information about a given subject. This definition sounds impressive but it does not explain how to reduce the number of accounts that are turned over for collection. In order to determine a solution, we must look at this issue from a different point of view. We will look at it from the standpoint of an individual account holder. In order to reduce the number of accounts turned over to collection agencies, there must be individual accountability.

What does individual accountability mean? It means that, if as a result of your actions there are consequences to be addressed, you will accept those consequences. The consequence of obtaining more credit than you can actually handle is being in debt, a very common problem. Once you are in debt, either you will turn it into someone else's problem (other consumers) or you will take responsibility and devise a plan to get out of debt. Devising a plan to get out of debt is what this book is all about.

The process of getting out and staying out of debt requires more than just throwing money at the problem. Being in debt is more of a result of behavior and a way of operating rather than a result of not earning enough money.

INTRODUCTION

Understanding this concept is the most important element to keep in mind throughout this book.

I will present very practical straight forward information for you to examine and put into use. I promise not to waste your time with unnecessary fluff. Another promise is there is no need to be an accountant or a financial wizard to follow this book. Keep in mind some of the information may not apply to your personal situation in a specific sense. However, you will find that all of the information is sound guidance. So let's get started. There are seven steps you must go through to become debt-free and to remain that way.

First step - In order to get out of debt, you must first realize you are in debt. This may sound like an obvious step, but not so. Just think about it this way, if it were so obvious, very few people would ever be in debt because they would fix the problem as soon as they became aware that their debt situation was on the road to becoming a problem.

Second step - You must understand exactly how you got into debt. Getting in debt does not just happen overnight. It takes time and effort. Once you understand how it happened, hopefully you will take aggressive measures to keep it from happening again. Remember the old saying, "Fool me once shame on you, fool me twice shame on me."

Third step - You must determine exactly how much debt you owe and determine the exact amount of your living expenses. This step is normally an eye opener. Most people in debt are not quite sure how much debt they actually have. We will solve this problem in the third step.

Fourth step - Simply, how much do you make? I will also ask you to identify the elements that determine how much your daily employment labor is worth.

Fifth step - You must determine the difference between what you owe and what you make. This may be another eye opener. I will discuss ways to improve your income picture if you find it necessary to do so.

Sixth step - You will devise a written payment schedule that will firmly set you on the road to becoming debt-free. There won't be any guessing involved. Once you have finished the sixth step, you will finally know exactly how long it will take for you to go through the entire process of getting out of debt. You will maintain and update this written schedule throughout the process and at any given point you will be able to check your progress.

Seventh step - You must understand how to stay out of debt.

Before we get started, round up a few sheets of paper, a pencil, a ruler and a calculator. I suggest taking your time while going through this book--there is no need to rush. The main objective is to clearly understand and address all of the contributing factors that caused your specific debt problem. Take time to ponder the different issues I will present. Good luck.

First Step

Realizing you are in debt

Admitting to yourself that you have a debt problem can be a difficult thing to do because to do so means that you will be responsible and do something about it or it means you will be irresponsible and do nothing. You have obviously made the decision to do something or at least you are thinking about it. Thinking about it is a major step.

Since you are thinking about it, where will this thinking lead you? For one thing you are reading this book. "Will this Alma Peterson person make a suggestion that I resort to eating only bread and water for the next five years and selling everything I own?" Of course not, that would be unrealistic and unreasonable. I will, however, offer some sound practical advice that should logically lead to a debt-free lifestyle.

1. Deciding to make some changes

It would be unrealistic for me to try to paint a painless, fluffy picture about how easy it will be to become debt-free. Let's face it, making the decision to rid yourself of debt will require some changes in the way you have been operating. Your spending habits will have to be adjusted. You may have to change your lifestyle for a period of time. Some lifestyle changes can be more drastic and more humbling than others.

While you don't have to eat bread and water, you may have to stop eating lunch out everyday. Instead of shopping-till-you-drop, you may have to shop only when it is a necessity. Instead of having the latest and greatest stereo - computer - laser - vision combination, you may have to settle for what you already have. Who knows, you may have to stick with your current mode of transportation for awhile, buses, taxicabs and trains included.

I know these may be harsh words and maybe you have never heard them before, but someone had to break the news. So prepare yourself mentally and make a commitment to stick with what ever it takes to obtain a debt-free lifestyle.

2. What does being in debt mean to you?

You say you are in debt. Does that mean if you only had more money you wouldn't be in debt? This is a common belief. Does this mean people who are rolling in dough are never in debt? The answer is no. We often read about wealthy people in the news who file for bankruptcy or have problems with the Internal Revenue Service. Being in debt is not just isolated to one economic group.

Most people categorize themselves as being in debt when they find it difficult or impossible to meet all of their financial obligations. The actual meaning of the word debt is an obligation or liability to pay or return something to another or others. Based on this definition almost everyone is in debt to some degree. But I will focus on the type of debt that makes it difficult or impossible for people to meet their financial obligations.

One of the things I hope you will understand after finishing this book is that the inability to meet financial obligations is not necessarily caused by a lack of money, but instead by another common problem. I'm not trying to say a lack of money is not a major factor of being in debt. But more so than a lack of money, a lack of planning has a great deal to do with the inability to meet financial obligations.

Think about it, would you have planned to get into debt? I didn't plan it that way. More than likely you didn't plan it that way either. We just didn't have a plan. That's okay, we have learned from that mistake. Although I did not plan to get into debt, I did plan to get out of debt and stay that way.

3. Fear of the unknown

One of the main factors that will keep people from thinking rationally about their debt situation is their drive to fit into a particular social mold. This mold compels us to try to present a certain image of ourselves to others. Many of us are guilty of this to a degree. We may live in a particular neighborhood, drive a certain type of car, eat at exclusive restaurants, shop at the most expensive department stores and a myriad of other idiosyncrasies. If we are unable to do these things that present a certain image, much of our time is preoccupied with trying to be able to do so. Not only do we attempt to present a certain image to others, we may also evaluate ourselves using the same criteria. We may find ourselves thinking more or less of ourselves based on the material things around us.

REALIZING YOU ARE IN DEBT

The question is, what do neighborhoods, cars, restaurants and expensive stores have to do with you as a person? Absolutely nothing at all. Of course, there is nothing wrong with desiring nice things and pleasant surroundings. The point I would like to make is you should always be able to distinguish youself from the purchased goods. You should not have the attitude that leads to the belief that you positively must do or have this or that thing in order to be happy and acceptable to others and to yourself. This type of thinking will ultimately lead to spending well beyond your means and experiencing an overall sense of unhappiness.

Another way to put this in perspective is to consider the countless number of different cultures and customs around the world. In almost every culture, there is something, whether it is a possession or position, that has some degree of prestige or disgrace associated with it. As you know, what may be everything to one group of people may be absolutely nothing to another group. For instance, somewhere on this planet there are people who are surrounded by servants every day of their lives. Although we may enjoy indulging in the niceties that way of life has to offer, most of us wouldn't think it is an absolute necessity to have servants. It may be a fantasy but certainly not a necessity.

Imagine someone who was having great financial difficulty, while at the same time supporting a team of 15 servants. What would you say to this person? You would say, "Get rid of the servants." This person would say to you,

"But how can I possibly live without my servants?" You would say, "It won't be that bad, I live without servants everyday. You'll get used to it."

So, if you are currently in debt but at the same time feeling anxious about the possibility of being deprived of future purchases, give yourself some time. You'll get used to the new way of operating.

4. Not all debt is equal

It would be naive to think most people could pay off a thirty-year mortgage within a couple of years--that is not the purpose of this book. Although you may not be able to pay off the mortgage any time soon, I do realize it may be a source of anxiety for you along with your other bills. Unless you decide to sell, and I'm not suggesting that you should, your mortgage payment will be with you for quite some time. However, unlike your credit cards and other loans, your mortgage represents a tangible, and hopefully, an appreciable asset. An asset that will be with you long after the other bills are gone.

On the other hand, credit cards and other loans represent that other debt. The debt we all want to bring under control. The debt that seems to linger around with no end in sight. You know, those precious things you just couldn't do without. Those things that are now causing your credit card balances to resemble a giant rolling snowball. Some of those things may not seem so precious to you now.

Regardless of whether you pay a mortgage or rent, the time needed to get rid of your debt will vary based on how much other debt you have. But how ever long it does take, once you have paid the final payment, you will have a heavy burden lifted from your shoulders. And, if you play your cards right, it will never happen again. Later, I will discuss how mortgages can be paid off years in advance once your other debts have been paid in full.

5. The stress of debt

The realization of debt can be stressful and depressing for some people. There may be bills that go unpaid and harassment from creditors. Hopefully that is not your situation yet. But if it is, do not let it get the best of you. Just remember, you can only do what you can do. The mere fact that you are reading this book means that you are taking steps to address your debt problem.

The stress of debt can cause physiological and psychological changes as well. By psychological changes, I am not trying to suggest that you are losing your mind. Instead, what I am saying is the mere act of thinking about your debt situation may cause you to feel anxious. You may not be able to sleep at night and your stomach may be in knots most of the time. The ringing of your phone may cause you to cringe. You may be irritable and short tempered. If you did not feel at least some anxiety about your debt situation, you wouldn't be taking the time to understand ways to remedy the problem.

6. Who's to blame?

It goes without saying that these physiological and psychological changes can have a negative impact on you and those around you. In fact, your job performance can also suffer as a result of your debt situation. It is clear that if your job performance is negatively impacted, you will have a brand new set of problems to deal with.
In general, you may find yourself wanting to blame someone else for the predicament you are in. No doubt, you may have had some assistance in building your empire of debt. I don't want to be insensitive, but whatever it was that caused your debt is now "water under the bridge." You can't do anything about that now. What ever caused your situation has happened and what has already happened can not be changed.

As the saying goes, "It is what it is." Although you cannot change what has happened, you can take aggressive measures to keep the same thing from happening in the future. Use your current situation as a learning experience.

I remember my first year of college--let's just say it was an expensive vacation. Although things did not go the way I would have liked, I did take out a hefty student loan for that year. At the time, I wanted to find someone to blame. But no amount of blaming would have changed the fact that I was the one who had taken out the student loan and it was my responsibility to pay it back.

7. Reaching out to others

To help cope with the stress of debt, you may want to consider discussing your situation with friends or family, especially if they are, or will be, directly affected by the debt. If you have children who are old enough to understand, ask them to suggest ways they will be able to help you reach your goal. By making your debt-free goal a family project, there may be less friction when some routine things are reduced or eliminated altogether. It also may keep your children from finding themselves in the same predicament years down the road.

There are financial counselors and advisors you may want to consider contacting. You can also talk to a minister or a counselor at a local church even if you are not a member. There are public mental health counselors as well. Check your local yellow pages under counseling services.

8. The attitude of avoidance

Make sure you communicate with your creditors. By creditors, I mean the company through which you actually have the account and/or the credit collection agency if an account has been turned over for collection. Many people who find themselves in debt will adopt the attitude of avoidance. They may stop answering the phone and may even use their children as a point of contact for creditors. It is almost as if they hope the problem will just magically disappear. Well, it does not work that way.

You need to attack the problem and take full responsibility. Taking responsibility means that you will not avoid your creditors. If you are avoiding your creditors, ask yourself a couple of questions:

1. Why do I avoid my creditors?
2. Will avoiding my creditors solve the problem?
3. When do I plan to contact my creditors?
4. What will I say when I do call?

You should spend some time thinking about your answers to these questions. If you are avoiding your creditors, you have probably convinced yourself this is the best way to handle the situation. Maybe you have not thought about it at all--you just automatically avoid having any contact with them.

9. Making efforts to contact creditors

Contrary to what you believe, talking with your creditors may even make you feel better about your overall debt circumstance. More than likely, someone has been trying to reach you and they have left their name and telephone number on several occasions. Surprise them and call back.
Explain that you are aware of the fact you owe them money and that you have every intention of repaying the amount in full. If you are experiencing a specific hardship, provide the details to the extent you feel comfortable. Provide the person with a general time frame they can expect to receive payment from you.
Get the person's full name and make a note of the date and time of the conversation. Tell them to feel free to call back if they have not heard from you by the specified date. At this point, you have somewhat diffused the situation. You may consider sending them a letter to make the conversation a part of your record. You also can request that they not call you anymore if that is your desire. Just remember, asking them not to call does not solve the problem. If another person from the same company calls within the same time frame, you can reference your previous

conversation.

The Federal Fair Debt Collection Practices Act of 1977 was enacted to protect individuals from unfair collection practices. If you feel you are being unduly harassed, ask the creditors if they are familiar with the above act. If the answer is no, request to speak with someone in charge. There are a few things you should know about the act. First, creditors should not call you before 8 a.m. or after 9 p.m.. Second, if you have requested in writing, they should not call you at work.

I suggest waiting until after you have finished this book and have a clear picture of your financial state before making a call to your creditors. Earlier I said you can only do what you can do. Well, contacting your creditors is one of the things you can do.

Although there is no guarantee, communicating with your creditors may even prevent a negative reporting to the credit bureau. If you already have a negative credit rating, don't worry about it. Just as purchased goods do not define who you are, neither does a credit rating. Regardless of your situation, if you do not communicate with your creditors, especially if they are trying to reach you, they have no idea of your intentions for payment. Later, I will discuss contacting your creditors for the purpose of requesting a monthly payment reduction.

If you have received a negative credit rating, there are ways to repair your credit rating. There are several books on the market that are devoted solely to repairing your credit. These books can be located in the personal finance section at your local bookstore or library. Although I will not discuss credit repairing in great detail, I will provide you with the names and addresses of the three predominate credit bureaus in the United States:

>Equifax Credit Information Systems
>Consumer Assistance Department
>P.O. Box 740241
>Atlanta, GA 30374-0241
>(404) 885-8000
>
>Trans Union Corporation
>Consumer Assistance Department
>P.O. Box 7000
>North Olmsted, OH 44070
>(312) 645-6000
>
>TRW Information Services
>Consumer Assistance Department
>P.O. Box 749029
>Dallas, TX 75374-9029
>(214) 235-1200, ext 251
>(714) 991-6000 (West Coast residents)

You always have the right to know the contents of your credit report and a right to file an addendum with these credit bureaus in order to explain your side of the story. So when creditors access any credit information relative to you, they will also be able to take into account your version of the facts.

10. Friends and family as creditors

Communicating with your creditors also includes communicating with any friends or family who may have given you a loan in the past. Unless they are experiencing some type of financial hardship as well, friends and family will probably be very understanding. But just as with your other creditors, your friends and family will have no idea of your intention for repayment if you do not discuss it with them. Discussing your repayment intentions goes hand in hand with being accountable.

Second Step

How did you get into debt?

Let's face it, no one really plans to get into debt, it just kind of happens that way. Well not quite. Most of us obtained our first credit card or loan to "Establish credit." We were told that was the thing to do. "You can't do anything without credit." Well, just how much credit do you need to do whatever it is you need to do? I don't think anyone has ever really asked and answered this question.

Some of us may have been rejected the first couple of times we applied for credit and, of course, some of us took those rejections personally. "How dare they reject me, I am a responsible person. I have a job." Some of us may have erroneously based our self-worth on whether some company granted us credit or not. If we only knew then what we know now.

1. That first credit card

What happened after we received that first credit account? Everybody and their family members wanted to give us credit. We may have even thought of calling those who rejected us to give them a second chance.

At first, the card was only going to be used for emergencies or maybe to rent a car when traveling. After a while, we started using it occasionally when we needed something right away and we didn't have the cash on us. The rest is history.

2. The 2nd, 3rd, 4th,...credit cards

Now, since we were still "establishing credit," we accepted everything offered to us. This is where the river of debt started. The water may have been smooth and calm at first. A few miles back you probably noticed that the current was starting to pick up a little but you could handle it. Before you realized what was going on, you had lost control of your credit boat. Now you are just fighting to stay in the boat and above water.

3. Interest rates

It is possible you paid very little attention to the interest rates of your first few credit cards. Some of the interest rates could have been as much as 22%. A number of the well known department stores especially fall into this category. Many of the bank cards are only slightly better.

The interest rate is the main reason why a department store or credit card company wants to grant you credit. It has nothing to do with how wonderful you are as a person. You are paying them for the privilege of buying stuff. They don't care what the stuff is or whether or not you can afford it. If you want merchandise and agree to pay the interest, you can buy it. It is as simple as that.

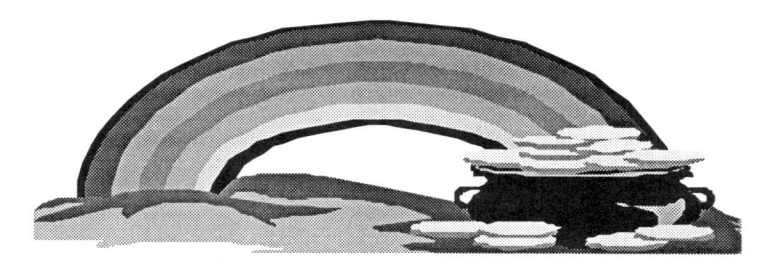

4. Credit card enticements

Many department stores, banks and a number of other credit card providers offer incentives to attract new card holders. You can get free gasoline, automobiles, airline miles, long-distance telephone calls, trips, meals for the hungry, and even cash back just for using a particular credit card. I am not saying there is anything wrong with any of these enticements, but the use of the cards should be carefully thought out. If not, you may find yourself holding five, ten, fifteen or more credit cards with substantial balances on each. Accepting additional credit cards just to obtain special incentives may not be in your best interest, especially if you are already holding several other cards.

Often, enticements justify why you must have a particular card. For example, for every $100 spent on merchandise, you can get a $10 gift certificate. "If you open an account today, you will receive this beautiful sterling silver serving tray." Or you may be able to buy one meal and get another one free if you use a particular card. After all, you will be saving money. Believe me, this is not how you want to make a habit of saving money.

you're the tops!

5. The valued customer category

    What happens after you have paid on your accounts a few times without delay is you become a "valued customer." As a valued customer, you are congratulated with an increased credit limit. The notification will read something like, "We are pleased to inform you that based on your remarkable payment history, we are increasing your available credit limit." What they are really saying is, "Since you are increasing our profit margin so much, we thought you would like more opportunities to donate to our cause."
    When you receive your increased limit, do you call them up and say, "Thanks but no thanks"? Of course not. Unfortunately, most people use the additional credit limit just because its there. That way of thinking must be changed if you ever plan to become debt-free. The ideal situation would be to pay all credit card balances at the end of each month. If everyone did that, credit cards would not be such a booming business. There would be less of an incentive for banks and other entities to issue cards.

6. Pre-approved credit applications

In addition to receiving increased credit limits, you are now receiving pre-approved credit applications in the mail every day. These can be very tempting especially if you find yourself needing a little cash at the time. All you have to do is sign the application and send it back. You may have "maxed-out" your other cards, but now you are back in business. Now you can pile up even more debt.

7. Cash advances

It is not uncommon for card holders to accept a new credit card for the sole purpose of obtaining a cash advance. The bank may have turned you down for a loan but, being the valued customer you are, you can get a cash advance for the full amount of your credit limit. Of course, cash advances are a lot more expensive for you than regular merchandise and service purchases. Normally you will pay higher interest rates as well as a substantial fee for the cash advance. The bottom line is, cash advances cost you more money. Avoid them if you can.

8. Haphazard spending

There is something about credit cards that give people the freedom to purchase items as if they are spending toy money. There is little or no planning involved even when making large purchases. Since most card holders do not keep a running ledger of their purchases, the results are often the same whether the purchases are large or small. The consequence of haphazard credit card spending is debt. Here are a few questions you should answer about your spending habits:

1. Do you spend haphazardly?
2. Do you spend money because of a particular mood you are in?
3. If so, what causes that mood?
4. Is the mood caused by certain people, places, events or circumstances?
5. Do you have to spend money or can you stop anytime you want?

The answers to these questions must be provided by you. That last question may sound like the type of question you would pose to a smoker, a drug user or anyone who is engaging in an activity that is obviously dangerous to his or her health. Haphazard spending can be detrimental to your overall well-being. If you are serious about getting out of debt, you need to attempt to identify the motivation behind your spending habits.

Your answer may be, "There is no hidden reason, I just like to shop, travel, entertain, eat out and whatever else I can do with my credit card." The truth of the matter is, if you are incurring new debt every month, but not paying your balances in full each month, you are spending what you don't have. You may say, "That's why I have credit cards."

The question is, "Where and when does it stop?" Do you have a plan to stop spending at a certain dollar amount or will you continue spending until you reach all of your credit limits? Have you even seriously thought about it at all? More than likely, not. And you are not alone. Unfortunately, most people who get in trouble with credit cards just don't think about the long term consequences of charging.

Let's stop and think a minute. Look around you and identify all of the items you have purchased on credit or have taken out loans to obtain. Include purchases like vacations, parties and other services. How many of those purchases were spur-of-the-moment purchases? How many of those purchases would you make if you could do it all over again? More than likely there are some things you would do differently.

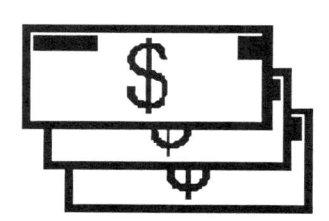

9. Paying the minimum amount

Paying the minimum amount due is great for your creditors but not so good for you. One day there is that rude awakening, "Hey this balance never seems to get any smaller." Prior to this revelation, you may have decided that you would cut back on the charging for a couple of months and pay down some of the balances. But you don't see much difference in the balances even though you are writing checks every month and you have not charged much lately.

What is going on? Maybe your account is not being credited properly. Once you are assured everything is fine with your account, you realize someone is making a large amount of money, thanks to your privilege to make purchases on credit.

You don't have much choice in the matter, especially if you are holding several credit accounts with substantial balances on each. As an example:

- One of your many credit cards has a balance of $2,700.
- The Annual Percentage Rate (APR) is 18.50%.
- Your monthly rate is about 1.54%. (Your monthly rate is your APR divided by 12.)
- Each card may vary, but let's assume that your minimum amount due for this month on this card is $81, which is 3% of the balance. (3% is commonly the industry standard)
- If you only pay the minimum amount due of $81.
- $41.58 is the amount of interest you will pay for this month.

- with only $39.42 going to reduce the principal balance from $2,700 to $2,660.58.

Clearly, if you had several cards with similar balances, the minimum amount due on each could be a substantial amount. If your income does not allow you to pay much more than the minimum amount due, it is clear that it will take years to pay those accounts down even if you did not make another purchase from this day forward. In fact, if we continue with the above example, if you only paid the minimum amount due every month, it would take 11 years and 9 months to pay-off that $2,700 balance, and that is without any additional purchases.

Of course, the credit card companies and department stores would just love it if you never paid any more than the minimum amount due because they get an unbelievable return on their money. If we found a savings account that would give us that much of a return on our money, we would put everything we had into that account. So, what do we do when we find ourselves in this situation? We have to come up with a plan.

Third Step

Exactly how much do you owe and what are your living expenses?

Now that you know what caused your debt, how do you start the process of getting out of debt? The purpose of the third step is to determine exactly how much you are spending each month. This includes what you owe to all of your creditors as well as your monthly living expenses. In this section, we will also try to get a handle on your monthly miscellaneous expenses.

We will start with the miscellaneous purchases. You will be surprised at how much is spent each day on miscellaneous items. The quick stop at the gourmet coffee stand before work everyday. The muffin at the donut shop. The magazine from the newsstand. The pizza to watch the game. The make-up party at your sister's house. The bread maker. If there is no specific plan in place to monitor miscellaneous purchases, these expenses can add up to a large amount.

The purpose for including the miscellaneous expenses is not to make you feel guilty for purchasing such things while in debt. Neither is the purpose to deprive you of those items. The purpose is to make you aware of where every penny is going. By knowing where every penny is going, you can make intelligent decisions about your spending, whether it is a miscellaneous purchase or otherwise. The goal here is for you to know whether or not it is practical to make a particular purchase based on your financial state at the time.

When determining all of your expenses, do not try to compile the list in your head because you will probably leave something out or make an error with the figures. Always write everything down. I have included some examples of ways you may want to track your spending.

EXACTLY HOW MUCH DO YOU OWE?

1. The total of all miscellaneous purchases

The first thing you want to do is to compile a list of your miscellaneous expenses. If possible, try to list miscellaneous expenses you have already incurred. Go through your daily routine and list all the things you can remember purchasing on a regular basis. List any food purchases that are not part of your regular grocery shopping. Regular grocery shopping also includes the periodic trips to the grocery store to purchase milk, bread, fruit, etc. Try to remember everything even if it was just a pack of gum. If you purchase tobacco products and alcoholic beverages, remember to include these items as well.

If you are not able to remember in detail the miscellaneous purchases you normally make during any given month, spend the next few weeks keeping a daily ledger of those expenses. This may sound silly and petty, but the truth of the matter is that it is possible to spend into the hundreds of dollars or more per month on miscellaneous purchases. If you are going to spend this amount of money, you should at least plan to do so. You can use a tiny note pad to gather this information. See Figure 3-1.

Figure 3-1 Sample of Miscellaneous Purchases

4 November

Grande cafe mocha	$2.25
4 pieces of Best Chocolates	$1.80
Salad take-out bar	$8.20
Diet Coke	.80
Magazine	$2.00
Order of fries & diet coke	$1.50
Pizza	$15.75
Total	$32.30

5 November

Grande cafe mocha	$2.25
Lunch at Husky's	$15.00
Yogurt cone	$1.20
Pack cheese crackers	.75
Diet coke	.80
Movie rental	$3.00
Alpha-hydroxy shampoo	$5.50
Total	$28.50

6 November

Grande cafe mocha	$2.25
Blueberry muffin	$1.00
Lunch at Chino's	$13.00
Photo processing	$10.00
Gummy bears	$1.50
Shoe sale	$75.56
Total	$103.31

EXACTLY HOW MUCH DO YOU OWE?

If you take the time to keep track of your miscellaneous purchases, you will see that these purchases can add up quickly. Most people with debt problems have no idea how much money they actually spend on a day-to-day basis. Eliminating this mode of operating is one of the changes you want to make if you plan to get out of debt and stay out.

Instead of buying coffee everyday, a comuter cup can be purchased and the coffee made at home. Taking a lunch to work instead of eating out can be a considerable savings. Favorite snacks can be purchased in multiple packs instead of individually. There are many ways to reduce miscellaneous spending.

Keep the record of your miscellaneous expenses handy because you will use this information later in step six.

2. The total of all living expenses

Next, compile a list of all of your living expenses. This list should include expenses such as mortgage/rent, utilities, auto insurance, groceries, water and sewer, garbage collection, etc. If you are a parent of school age children, include expenses for child care, child support, lessons and other activities.

Do not forget things such as gasoline for your vehicle, dry-cleaning, cable, telephone, maid service, lawn service, pharmacy bill, etc. Don't leave anything out, because you may be able to cancel or reduce some items to improve your monthly income. You can use your checkbook ledger to assist you in compiling your list of living expenses.

It is important to be reasonable and practical when listing the amounts for things such as groceries, child care and other necessities. If you have to estimate the amount for these items, guess on the high side rather than the low side. For instance, don't try to convince yourself that you will cut back on your grocery bill by surviving on peanut butter and jelly sandwiches. You will only become discouraged if you cannot keep such an unreasonable and unrealistic goal. For this list, make four columns:

"Expense"
"Due-date"
"Amt. due"
"Balance"

The "Balance" column for the living expenses should be "0" unless you have past due amounts. See Figure 3-2.

3. The total of all credit cards and other debts

Continuing with the same list, tabulate all of your credit cards and other debts. As with your living expenses, each credit account should be listed separately with the due dates, the amount due and the balance. If you have more than one of the same type of credit card, list each card by

EXACTLY HOW MUCH DO YOU OWE?

name. For example, "Chase Visa" and "Security Visa."

If you have your monthly statements handy, use them to accurately reflect your balances instead of estimating. If you don't know the actual balance, list an approximate balance for now. Of course, as your monthly statements come in, adjust your written notes to reflect the accurate amounts.

Do not forget to include loans you may have received from friends and relatives. Although you may be able to make arrangements to pay these off later, you don't want to forget they exist.

Write the total of all expenses on your worksheet. Don't despair if the total of everything causes you to feel a little light-headed, things will get better.

4. Create a simple filing system

If you are not doing so already, start saving copies of the monthly statements corresponding to all of your accounts, at least until you have made the final payment. Develop a filing system for your statements. It does not have to be anything fancy or complicated. 9 inch by 12 inch envelopes or accordion files will be sufficient. Just simply identify the account name on the outside of the envelop or accordion section.

Keeping the statements in one location will help you become more organized and, at the same time, the statements will help track your progress. Being more organized is the main purpose for

37

saving the statements.

People in debt tend to be a little sloppy relative to the bills they receive in the mail. There is no particular location for the bills when they come in. A few might be on the kitchen counter, others in the bedroom and others under a stack of magazines. Being unorganized is one of the behaviors that tends to foster being in debt. At any given point, you have no idea of exactly who you owe or how much. One day you receive a past-due notice in the mail. "OOPS, I forgot about this one" or "I thought I had already paid this."

At my house, we keep track of the current month's bills by placing them in a decorative fixture we have hanging on our kitchen wall. On the outside of the envelope, we write the date the bill should be mailed in order for it to reach its destination by the due date. The bills are then filed in chronological order based on the dates we have written on the envelopes. The envelopes are filed in a manner that keeps them visible to us whenever we walk by.

In addition to saving the old statements and arranging them in chronological order, find a location to hold your current month's bills where they will always stare you in the face. By taking these steps, you will begin to change your organizational habits for the better. Wherever you decide to keep the current and old statements, be mindful of protecting your accounts from unauthorized use.

EXACTLY HOW MUCH DO YOU OWE?

Figure 3-2 Sample Worksheet of Mthly Expenses
Monthly Expenses

Expense	Due Date	Mthly Amt. due	Balance
Rent/Mortg.	1st	$700	0
Gas & Electric	17th	$80	0
Car insurance	1st	$125	0
Water & Sewer	15th	$65	0
Telephone	22nd	$80	0
Cable	15th	$56	0
groceries	bi wkly	$130	0
CM Visa	18th	$60	$2,000
Sec Pac MC	3rd	$50	$1,700
NCS Visa	2nd	$80	$2,700
HC Dept. Store	10th	$30	$1,000
WC Furniture	28th	$25	$800
Student loan	1st	$50	$650
Car loan	15th	$364.64	$10,000
Gasoline	mthly	$72	0
dry cleaning	bi wkly	$40	0
Eating out	mthly	$250	0
Manicurist	bi wkly	$40	0
Other entertain.	mthly	$100	0
Car wash	mthly	$56	0
	Total	$2,453.64	$18,850

Monthly Income - $1,940.80
Extra Income - 0

Fourth Step

How much is your income?

How much you are paid and how often are important pieces of information for this fourth step. Is your income set or does it vary from one pay period to the next? If your income is fixed, it will be a little easier for you to develop a financial plan than if it varies. For the purpose of this fourth step, if your income does vary, use the least amount you always receive to calculate your monthly income. Any amount above and beyond the least amount should be listed as extra income. Later I will discuss how to take advantage of any extra income. On the other hand, I will also discuss options to take when you always bring home less than your monthly obligations. Of course, it goes without saying that if you always bring home less than what your obligations are, there are some other things you need to consider. But I will discuss that later.

For now, list all sources of income on a sheet of paper. Don't forget things like bonuses, commissions, dividends and tips. If these extra sources of income are not always received on a monthly basis, list them as "Extra Income."

Once you have finished calculating your actual monthly income, write it on the "Monthly Expenses Worksheet" from step three.

1. How often are you paid each month?

Are you paid weekly, biweekly or monthly? If you are only paid once per month, careful planning is necessary to ensure you don't run out of funds before the next payday. Do you live in a double income family or will you be depending on your single salary? Whatever your circumstance, there is a plan that will work for you.

2. A side note

Before we get into the differences between your expenses and your income, I would like to spend some time on a side issue. I would like to ask a question. To some the question could be totally irrelevant and to others it may just hit home. I think it is an important question. However, it is a question that is very rarely considered by millions of people who could surely benefit from simply pondering the question.

"What is the question?" you ask. The question is, what factors determine your income? "What kind of question is that?" you ask. Think about it. Is your income based on how exhausted you feel after eight hours on the job? Is it how well you are dressed? Does it have anything to do with how much physical labor you expend while on the job? Is it the training you received after being hired on the job? Is it based on some type of educational degree or certificate you obtained before being hired?

The answers to this question are numerous. It is very possible that your answer is not included in the list of answers above. The reason for asking the question, however, is this basic philosophy I have. I believe, if you have to leave your home everyday to go out and work somewhere for eight hours, five days a week, you should make as much money as possible while out there. Of course, I am referring to legal employment and you should enjoy whatever it is you are doing. And from a humanity standpoint, your pursuit for advancement should be based on your abilities and not an effort to devalue those around you in order to make yourself more attractive.

From this philosophy, one could get the erroneous perception that I am only interested in money. Not true. I don't doubt there are those who would work on their jobs for no charge because they love their work that much. If more of us had that luxury, we might even do the same thing. But since this is not the case most of the time, the rest of us work everyday to make it possible for us and our families to live under a roof and to partake in life's other necessities and pleasures. So I say again, if you have to go to work anyway, make the most of your valuable time while out there.

How do you do that? Ask yourself, "What factors of my employment duties dictate to my employer what the dollar value each hour of my labor is worth?" The next question, "Is there anything I can do that will make each hour of my time more valuable to my employer than it is right now?" Another question is, "What can I do that will make my precious time more valuable to another employer?" This other employer could be you as your own employer, or it could be some other company or entity.

Another way to think about the basic question is to imagine that you are out shopping for a special lamp. You don't really know exactly what type of lamp yet but when you do find it, there won't be any doubt in your mind that you have found your lamp. There may be other lamps that are cheaper and possibly more practical, but you will pay the extra money to get the lamp you really want.

Now imagine yourself as the lamp and your employer or potential employer as the one shopping for the lamp. Based on the lamp example, there needs to be something different about you that will allow you to stand out in the sea of lamps. This is not to say you have to be the fanciest lamp or the most expensive lamp. But there needs to be something that says, "Hey, I'm your lamp."

I am sure you have heard the phrase, "a dime-a-dozen." If you are able to purchase something for a dime-a-dozen, more than likely you would think you were getting a pretty good deal, or maybe not, depending on what it is. You certainly wouldn't pay twenty-cents-a-dozen for the same thing. The item is so common and plentiful that the seller can not afford to raise the price if he expects to continue to sell the item.

Try to view your employment in the same light. You cannot reasonably expect to demand a higher value for your labor if all of the identical labor around you is demanding or settling for less. There may be a number of avenues available to you that would allow you to increase the dollar value of your employment time.

Technical schools, training courses, college courses, seminars, books, etc., are great starting points. Some of these avenues may be available at no cost. But, at a minimum, deciding to participate in any of these activities will take time to complete and a commitment to follow through.

Don't let the length of time required to complete an activity dissuade you from considering it. Just look at your life as an example. If you are like me, when you look back over your life, the years can actually seem like months--time really moves fast. Whatever your decision, you have to weigh any possible benefits based on your specific situation.

Fifth Step

What is the difference between your expenses and what you make?

    Hopefully what you owe and spend each month does not exceed your monthly income, but if it does you now know that fact. Your financial picture is right before your eyes and you can no longer simply "wing it." Maybe this is the first time you have really taken a look at your financial picture. You are not alone.

Because credit is so accessible, it is not uncommon for people to unconsciously create large sums of debt without planning to do so. Whether or not you have made the final decision to embark on the mission of becoming debt-free, you should always be aware of where all of your money is going each month. Being aware of your financial situation will discourage haphazard purchasing and encourage careful planning.

1. Making the commitment to move forward

If your monthly income is more than or equal to your monthly expenses, moving to the next step will be a breeze. You will simply need to make a commitment not to incur any more unnecessary expenses during your journey of becoming debt-free. This is easier to say than to do, but think about this one fact. Right now you are in debt and you don't like it. If you could turn back the clock, and you knew then what you know now, would you travel down the same road? Would you incur the same debt in the same manner? Hopefully, your answer is no.

Undoubtedly, some of your debt may have been caused by circumstances beyond your control. But it is possible that the largest portion of your debt was caused by a lack of planning and poor judgment. Now that you have the opportunity to get out of debt, make the responsible decision not to incur any new debt. If you can't bring yourself to destroy all of your

DIFFERENCE BETWEEN EXPENSES AND INCOME

credit cards, at least take one small step in that direction. Just remove your credit cards from your wallet and lock them up at home in a safe place. In fact, a friend of mine just took this very step.

By removing your credit cards from your wallet, they are not as accessible. After you have done this for awhile, maybe you will develop enough nerve to destroy at least one card and then another and then another. Whether or not you decide to destroy all of your cards is up to you. Only you know the weaknesses you have with credit cards. Only you know if one day you will be able to use credit cards in a manner that does not leave you drowning in debt. You will have some weak moments along the way, just don't allow those moments to cause you to give up your quest to become debt-free.

2. What happens when you spend more than what you make?
or
How can you improve your monthly income?

If your monthly expenses exceed your income, or if you would like to improve your monthly income, exactly what do you do next? The first thing you should do is take another look at your "Monthly Expenses Worksheet." One of the reasons for listing every possible expense you could think of, is to be able to readjust your income to the positive side, if necessary.

Look at the "Monthly Expenses Worksheet" and determine what can be adjusted. For instance, first look at all of the items you would consider recreational and then total the amount of those items. Don't worry, the recreational items are not the only items we will examine.

The next category of items to look at is the things that are nice to do but not necessarily a necessity. This would include items such as the manicurist, auto detailing and the extra channels on your cable bill. Also, make sure you did not list an item as a monthly expense when you don't actually pay that bill each month. An example of this type of bill would be auto insurance or water and garbage collection.

If you did list a bill as a monthly expense and it really is a bill you only pay every other month, divide the amount due by the appropriate number of months and adjust the monthly amount due. See figure 5-1 for an example. This will allow you to lower your monthly amount due. Ideally, you want to evenly distribute all of your expenses in this manner. I will discuss the equal distribution of monthly expenses in more detail later in step six.

Figure 5-1 shows examples of how the monthly income can be adjusted more to the positive side of the scale if certain items are readjusted or eliminated for a period of time. As stated earlier, there is no need to force yourself on a diet of bread and water but you may need to make some changes.

DIFFERENCE BETWEEN EXPENSES AND INCOME

Figure 5-1 Expenses Readjustment

Water & Sewer $130 divided by 2 = $65

Eating out = $250 per month

Other entertainment = $100

Car wash = $56

Manicurist = $40

Cable movie and sports channels = $20
(if these two channels are removed the bill would be $36 instead of $56.)

Since no two financial pictures are exactly the same, you will have to decide what your priorities are. If you simply cannot bring yourself to eliminate some of your miscellaneous monthly expenses, or no amount of readjusting will help, there are other options.

Using your savings - One might ask, how could someone be in debt and have a savings account all at the same time? You would be surprised. There are those who will pay the high interest on credit cards and loans rather than touch their savings. They are saving for that rainy day. If this scenario describes you, it is now raining. I'm not suggesting you should use every penny in your savings account. But if you are able to readjust your income back to the positive side of the scale by paying off one or two bills, I suggest using your savings to do so. The 2-3% interest one receives on a savings passbook does not begin to approach the 21% interest one pays on a credit account. It simply does not pay to save at practically zero percent interest if you are turning around to pay double digit interest on your credit accounts.

Cashing in stocks and bonds - This is another option that may readjust your monthly income picture so that it is more or equal to your monthly expenses. Even if the stocks are somewhat depressed and maybe the bonds have not matured yet, they are still worth something. You may be able to pay off one or two credit accounts. But you wouldn't want to do this if your stock yields are higher than the interest on your credit accounts.

Liquidating part of your IRA - Just as with any stocks or bonds, your IRA (Individual Retirement Account) is cash that belongs to you. Of course, there are financial penalties associated with early withdrawal, but it is cash available to you.

Remember, my purpose here is for you to examine all of your options. The decision to use your savings, to sell stocks and/or bonds or to liquidate your IRA is a personal one. If you need help making a final decision relative to taking one of these options, you should consult a financial advisor and present all of the facts about your financial profile.

Taking a short-term extra job is another option to consider.

>Uh oh! "She finally said it."
>"I knew it would be something ridiculous."
>"I can't work a second job because I have too many other things going on."
>"I'm too old to work a second job."
>"I'm too young to work a second job."
>"Where will I find this second job?"
>"There are some things I just will not do."

Taking an extra job is just another option. If you truly want to become debt-free without incurring new debt, you need to examine all of your options. If you are obligated to pay out more than you are making, it is clear something has to be done.

A second job does not have to be something you must do every day of the week. For example, my last semester in college was a fairly heavy load, but there was no way I wanted to stay in school one more semester. I checked around and found one of the most expensive restaurants I could find. I wanted it to be expensive because the tips would be sizable. I was able to get a job working Friday nights, all day Saturday and from Noon through closing on Sunday. At the time, that was my only income. The tips were enough to cover all of my expenses.

The purpose of taking a second job is to work long enough to pay off the least amount of debt that will ultimately allow you to meet your obligations with your primary employment alone. Maybe one month will be long enough for you to reach that goal. Maybe two months, it all depends on your personal circumstances.

For various reasons, you may be at a point in your life where you can not see yourself working an extra job. You may be concerned about what others will think. Maybe you do not have the energy to work an extra job.

If the answer is not taking a second job, you may need to look for another job altogether--one that will allow you to meet your expenses. I understand that this is easy to say, but not necessarily easy to do. We have all heard that times are hard right now and good paying jobs are scarce. As with everything else, a job change is another option to think about.

An unconventional option

This next option may seem a little unconventional but it is an option to consider that may enable you to pay off some of your debt. I'm sure you are familiar with or at least have heard of pawn shops. People pawn things by exchanging personal belongings as collateral in return for loans. When the loan is repaid to the pawn shop, with interest of course, the personal belongings are returned to the owner.

No, I am not about to suggest that you should pawn all of your possessions at a pawn shop. What I do suggest, however, is a similar arrangement with friends, family, or possibly co-workers.

As an example, let's say you own a superduper size TV and a regular size TV, and at the present time you are making less than your monthly expenses. Let's assume that if you could pay off just one credit card that has a balance of about $1,000, you would be able to pay all of your monthly obligations with your regular salary.

Instead of pawning your superduper TV to a pawn shop, pawn it to a friend or a family member. Especially if you know of someone looking to purchase an item that you just happen to own. If you can do without certain pieces of your property for awhile, pawning to friends and family can be an excellent way to generate needed cash. What you are really doing is obtaining a secured loan.

Continuing with the superduper TV as an example, essentially you would give the TV to a friend in exchange for an amount of money you have both agreed upon. If you desire, you can specify a certain amount of time and other conditions for the arrangement. If possible, make the agreement in writing. It would be nice if you could receive the full amount of the agreement in one lump sum but, if not, other arrangements can be made. Once you return the money, your TV will be returned to you. Hopefully, your friends and family would not charge any interest.

If you decide to make this type of an arrangement, always try to obtain a fair market value for the item being pawned. If you have owned the item for a couple of years, you want to take that into account. You want to get the fair market value for a couple of reasons. First, if for some reason you are not able to repay the loan, the person holding your property is not out any money. On the other hand, if some unfortunate mishap takes place and your property is damaged beyond repair, you received a fair value for your property at the time of the initial agreement.

A pawn arrangement between friends and family should benefit all involved. The friends and family are able to help out a loved one in debt while benefiting at the same time. The person in debt is being responsible by thinking of innovative ways to solve his or her own debt problem by not transferring the problem to others. Often times when unsecured loans are obtained from friends and family, the repayment of that loan can tend to be seriously delinquent or never repaid at all. By pawning personal property, it is clear that you have an interest in repaying the amount in full. Figure 5-2 is an example of how a pawn agreement could be drafted.

Figure 5-2 Sample Pawn Agreement

Pawn Agreement

This Agreement is hereby entered into this _____ day of _____,19____, between

Your Name
_____
Street Address   City   State   Zip code

hereinafter called Owner of The Property, and Name of person taking your property

_____
Street Address   City   State   Zip code

hereinafter called the Holder of The Property.

The said parties, for the consideration hereinafter mentioned, hereby agree to the following:

1. The Owner of The Property shall provide the property described as Description of the property hereinafter referred to as The Property.

DROWNING IN DEBT? GET OUT AND STAY OUT!

to The Holder of The Property for a period of ___list the time-frame if desired___ in exchange for ___the amount___.

  2. At the end of the time-frame specified above, the Owner of The Property shall return a total of ___the amount___ to The Holder of The Property at which time The Holder of The Property will return The Property to The Owner of The Property.

  3. Unless a written supplemental agreement was reached between The Owner of The Property and The Holder of The Property, The Holder of The Property agrees to accept ownership of The Property as payment in full in the event The Owner of The Property expresses the inability to pay the specified amount for The Property.

  4. In the event The Property is damaged while in the custody of The Holder of The Property, The Holder of The Property will take necessary steps to repair The Property. If The Property cannot be repaired, The Holder of The Property agrees to retain The Property and relieve the Owner of The Property of the debt in the amount of ___the amount___.

_____   _____
Witness as to The Owner of The Property   Owner of The Property

_____   _____
Witness as to The Holder of The Property   Holder of The Property

DIFFERENCE BETWEEN EXPENSES AND INCOME

Requesting a payment reduction - Earlier in step one I mentioned that you may be able to contact some of your creditors and discuss different payment options. I will carry that point a little further here.

Imagine you have examined your "Monthly Expenses Worksheet." You have several credit cards and you have discovered you just don't have enough monthly income to pay all of your credit card bills every month. So now each month, you are picking and choosing which bill will be late for that month.

Instead of using the "picking" and "choosing" method, try to arrange a lower payment with one or two of your creditors. Maybe you'll only need to make this arrangement with one creditor. Granted the creditor may place a temporary or permanent freeze on your account, but since you are not using the card anyway, that's okay.

The creditor should be more than willing to work with you, especially if you contact them before your account becomes a problem. Creditors are aware that account holders can experience financial hardships from time-to-time. When making your initial request, it is a good idea to ask to speak with a supervisor in the credit department. By speaking with a supervisor, you may not have to repeat the details of your finances a second time.

Explain to the supervisor that due to some unforeseen financial hardship, you would like to request a reduction in your monthly payment. Don't feel it is necessary to embellish the story.

Remember it is what it is. Explain that you have every intention of repaying the full amount but at the present your finances are very limited. They may inquire as to the specific cause of your hardship. For instance, they may want to know if you have been laid-off or fired from your job. It is up to you how much detail to go into.

If you are able to arrange a payment reduction, obtain the full name, title and mailing address of the person to whom you spoke. After your telephone conversation or meeting with the credit supervisor, you should send a letter just to document your conversation. Prior to ending your conversation, explain that you would like to follow up your conversation with a letter. It is a good idea to send the letter registered mail and request that it be placed in your file. Figure 5-3 is a sample letter of a request for a payment reduction.

Requesting a deferment of payment- If you have student loans, you may also be able to request a deferment of payment. A deferment gives you a moratorium from making payments for a specified number of months. Keep in mind it is possible that the interest may not be deferred. Requesting a deferment must be done in writing. Contact your student loan repayment facility to determine if a deferment is an option available to you. Figure 5-4 is a sample request for deferment.

DIFFERENCE BETWEEN EXPENSES AND INCOME

Figure 5-3 Sample Payment Reduction Request

Your return address

January 25, 1997

Jane Doe, Credit Manager
ABC Department Store
123 Maine Ave
Anywhere, US 12345

Re: Payment reduction request

Dear Ms Doe:

Per our telephone conversation on January 24th, you granted a payment reduction for my account number 654321, from $80 per month to $40 per month effective February 1997. If my financial situation improves, I will resume my normal monthly payment. Please place of copy of this letter in my file for future reference. Thank you very much for your assistance.

Sincerely

_____

Figure 5-4 Sample Request for Deferment

Your return
address

January 30, 1997

Julie Mae Student Loans
P.O. Box 8910
Appleville, US. 23456

To whom it may concern:

Pursuant to your deferment option, I am requesting a deferment relative to my student loan account number 615243. Due to a current financial hardship, I am unable to make the scheduled monthly payments. Please notify me in writing of your decision. Thank you for your consideration.

Sincerely
_____

An option to consider wisely- Although I am somewhat reluctant to mention this next option, it is nevertheless an option. You can shop around for lower credit card interest rates and transfer your balances. You have to be careful when doing this for a couple of reasons. First, you need to make sure the transfer of a balance is not considered a cash advance. If it is, you may not be able to take advantage of the advertised low interest rate. So, do your homework.

DIFFERENCE BETWEEN EXPENSES AND INCOME

In a addition to my concern about the interest rates, I am concerned about making this recommendation because your old credit card now has the full credit limit available at your disposal. For some people, exercising this option is not a problem. They will get the new credit card and take advantage of the lower interest rate to improve their debt status. There is no problem saying good-bye to the old card. But for others this option is like recommending that the alcoholic drink wine rather than hard liquor in order to stop drinking. If you are familiar with the affects of alcohol on alcoholics, you realize the wine option is not any better than the original situation.

If you decide to take a new credit card, you must be sure to cancel the old card as soon as possible. If you don't believe you will have the willpower to cancel the old card, don't take this option. Without a doubt, you will eventually use your old card.

Requesting an interest rate reduction on a current card - In addition to shopping around for new credit cards with better interest rates, you may be able to convince your current credit card company to reduce your interest rate. The credit card business is very competitive and they may reduce your interest rather than risk losing your business to another company. A good time to try to get an interest rate reduction is when you receive the bill with your annual renewal fee. While you are at it, why not ask that the annual fee be waived also. It does not hurt to ask. Contact your customer service representative to make these requests. You can normally find that telephone number on the back of your card or on the monthly bill.

The option that may not solve the problem - Bankruptcy. I personally do not consider this an option. I am a firm believer in experiencing the consequences of our actions. "Quick fixes" are usually temporary. People in debt are normally in that situation due to some decisions they have made on their own. The decisions that sometimes result in personal debt are not necessarily directly related to using credit cards and incurring other debt. For instance, the decision could have been the lack of a decision to have a savings program years ago. Another decision could have been the decision not to prepare for a better paying job when the opportunity presented itself. There are a number of avenues that lead to being in debt.

Feeling the consequences of debt is a very effective deterrent to not ever being in debt again. It is a growing process. If you are bailed out of debt, what incentive is there to do things differently in the future. It is easy to say, "If I file for bankruptcy this one time, I will never let this happen again." If filing for bankruptcy is your option to getting out of debt, you have probably used this same rationale as justification for obtaining a loan some time in your past. "If I could just get this loan from the bank (or from a relative), I can get myself together from this point on." Did it work? No. It was too easy.

DIFFERENCE BETWEEN EXPENSES AND INCOME

More than likely it did not work because you did not examine the reasons that necessitated your getting the loan in the first place. That is what this book is all about. Yes, you want to get out of debt, but you want to get out of debt forever, not temporarily. As I have said before, there are those uncontrollable circumstances which will cause a major financial hardship. That can happen--that's life.

However, imagine this following scenario. There are two individuals who are making roughly the same salary. For whatever reason, they both hit "rock-bottom" financially at the same time. Prior to this happening, one of the two individuals always had problems managing money. He was always running out of money before the next payday. On the other hand, the other person was a great money manager. There was never a need to go without eating as a result of being out of money.

Now imagine both of these individuals are in luck. Some nice person has decided to give them each $50,000 in cash to get back on their feet. What do you think will happen to each individual?

More than likely the one who was always having problems with money will continue to have problems. Of course, he or she will purchase a new car and maybe some new furnishings but it will eventually happen again. He or she will be in debt all over again.

However, the other individual will use the money to his or her advantage. In fact this person will probably end up in a more favorable financial position than before. This person will use the money to pay off his or her debt rather than make new purchases. This person might even start a savings account or other investment with any remaining amount.

The important point here is that being in debt is not necessarily just a result of a lack of money, but rather a result of a way of thinking and operating. This way of thinking and operating includes haphazard spending, a lack of planning, financial irresponsibility, etc. Regardless of what it is called, it all leads to being in debt. Although it is not flattering to be described by any of these labels, you do want to be honest about what caused your debt predicament. So, if you want to get out of debt once and for all, a "quick fix" is not the solution.

Sixth Step

The process of getting out of debt

The first five steps were relatively straight forward. You now understand the "hows" and the "whys" of the debt process. You didn't plan to get into debt, but you have decided to make the necessary changes to do things differently in the future. You know what you have to work with because your financial picture is now clear. It is time to start getting out of debt. Aren't you excited?

The sixth step is where "the rubber meets the road." Once you have completed this step, you will be able to calculate the exact month each and every one of your credit accounts will be paid off, whereas before you had no idea. You were just writing checks every month with no end in sight. Now you know there is light at the end of the tunnel. Even if you can't see it yet, you know the light is there and it is coming your way.

1. Separating your monthly paychecks

We will start this process of getting out of debt by separating your monthly paychecks on paper. If you are paid four times per month, take two sheets of paper and divide each sheet into two halves using a pencil. If you are paid twice, divide one sheet of paper into two halves. If you are only paid once per month leave the paper blank. See figure 6-1 for an example. The example shown represents two paychecks per month. The purpose of this exercise is to begin developing a personalized payment schedule just for you.

In the top left corner of each of the divided sections, write first, second, third or fourth paycheck to indicate the order in the month each paycheck is received. Additionally, for each payday per month, write the approximate date of the month the check is received and the amount. For example, if your first check of the month is received around the third day of each month, write "Dte Rcvd - 3rd" just below where you have written "First paycheck." Write the amount of the check on the same line as "Dte Rcvd."

THE PROCESS OF GETTING OUT OF DEBT

Remember, if your check varies, write the least amount you always receive. If you receive other paychecks on a regular basis such as from a part time job, combine those with your corresponding regular paychecks.

The next thing you want to do is to divide your rent or mortgage by the number of paychecks you receive each month and write, "Rent" or "Mortgage" under each paycheck with the divided amount. For example, if your monthly rent is $700, divide that amount by the number of checks you receive each month. So if you receive two checks the divided amount is $350. Write $350 under both paychecks.

All of this may seem elementary, however, it is necessary. In the future, if you receive a raise or for some reason your income decreases, adjust your payment schedule to reflect the accurate amount.

Figure 6-1 Sample for two Paychecks Received

First Paycheck	1997 Jan	Feb	Mar
Dte Rcvd - 1st	970.40		
Rent - 1st	350		

Second Paycheck	Jan	Feb	Mar
Dte Rcvd - 15th	970.40		
Rent - 1st	350		

2. Minimum amount due

In the second step, I discussed paying the minimum amount due on credit card bills as one of the unforgiving reasons we accumulate large credit card balances. Here in the sixth step the minimum amount due has a new meaning. It now means this is where you start getting out of debt. Whatever your minimum payment is today on all of your credit card accounts, you need to make a commitment that from this day forward, you will not pay any less than that amount. The minimum amount due on your statements will start to reduce, but you will continue to pay at least the amount you are paying today. Just remember, the more you are paying in excess of the minimum amount due, the less the credit card company is making from you. If you do continue using one credit card after you have paid all of your credit cards in full, your goal will be to pay your balance in full each month.

3. Focusing on your lowest balance

Now that the amount you are paying on credit card balances will remain constant from month to month, your focus should be on the lowest credit card or loan balance you have. Of course, loan agreements are different from credit cards in that the monthly payments for loans are normally set throughout the life of the loan. But for the purpose of this exercise, include loan balances when determining the lowest balance of all of your accounts.

Focusing on the lowest balance will enable you to speed-up the process of getting out of debt. Notice, I said you will be focusing on the lowest balance. You might ask, "Shouldn't I first focus on the credit card with the highest interest rate?" That is a good question. I look at the situation like this, the process of getting out of debt is like being on a diet. You have to start somewhere. If you are trying to loose 150 pounds, it would be nice to loose 50 pounds during the first week of the diet; however, that would be an unrealistic goal, resulting in discouragement. If loosing 50 pounds in the first week was your goal, you would probably give up before getting started.

Because I don't want anyone to give up, we will start with the lowest balance. As I mentioned earlier, you do have the option of shopping around for better interest rates. Now, once you have finished paying off your lowest balance, the other balances will seem to start melting away. The balances will appear to melt away because, in addition to paying off the lowest balance, you will maintain a set payment on all of your other monthly payments, even though the minimum amount due is less than your actual payment.

Once your lowest balance is paid in full, you are then able to take that monthly payment and apply it toward the monthly payment of the second lowest balance. Once the second lowest balance is paid in full, that payment is then applied to the third lowest balance. The monthly payment you will be paying on the third lowest balance, in addition to the regular payment, will

THE PROCESS OF GETTING OUT OF DEBT

consist of the payments that were being paid on the original lowest and second lowest balances.

Once you have finished paying off a few balances and adding those payments to the next lowest balance, your increased payment is fairly substantial. Continue this process until you have applied the increased payment to all accounts and all balances are zero. Later you will see illustrations of how this process works.

4. Monthly due dates

Remember in the third step you listed all monthly expenses and the due dates. Take another look at your "Monthly Expenses Worksheet" paying particular attention to the "Due date" column. Depending on your personal situation, most of your bills may be due around the same time of the month or they may be spread out. If for instance most of your bills are due around the same time and you are paying them that way, you are probably running out of money before the next payday, or some bills are late or not paid at all. Instead of allowing the due dates to dictate to you when to pay the bills, use the due dates to your advantage.

On scratch paper, separate all of your bills and other expenses by the due dates and match those bills with the dates of your paychecks. Use scratch paper because you may need to rearrange some bills to make things more equitable. Use your "Monthly Expenses Worksheet" as a guide. See figures 6-2 and 6-3 for examples.

Figure 6-2 Sample Worksheet of Mthly Expenses

Expense	Due Date	Mthly Amt. due	Balance
Rent/Mortg. ✓	1st	$700	0
Gas & Electric ✓	17th	$80	0
Car insurance ✓	1st	$125	0
Water & Sewer ✓	15th	$65	0
Telephone ✓	22nd	$80	0
Cable ✓	15th	$56	0
groceries	bi wkly	$130	0
CM Visa ✓	18th	$60	$2,000
Sec Pac MC ✓	3rd	$50	$1,700
NCS Visa ✓	2nd	$80	$2,700
HC Dept. Store ✓	10th	$30	$1,000
WC Furniture ✓	28th	$25	$800
Student loan ✓	1st	$50	$650
Car loan ✓	15th	$364.64	$10,000
Gasoline	mthly	$72	0
dry cleaning	bi wkly	$40	0
Eating out	mthly	$250	0
Manicurist	bi wkly	$40	0
Other entertain.	mthly	$100	0
Car wash	mthly	$56	0
	Total	$2,453.64	$18,850

THE PROCESS OF GETTING OUT OF DEBT

Fig. 6-3 Sample Equal Distribution Scratch paper

First paycheck - 1st	$970.40
Rent - 1st	350.00
Water & Sewer - 15th	65.00
Cable - 15th	56.00
HC Dept Store - 10th	30.00
Sec Pac MC - 3rd	50.00
Telephone - 22nd	80.00
CM Visa - 18th	60.00
Car loan - 15th	<u>182.32</u>
(car loan was divided)	
Total	$873.32

Remaining misc. $97.08
(Includes amount for groceries)

Second Paycheck - 15th	$970.40
Rent - 1st	350.00
Gas & Electric - 17th	80.00
Car insurance - 1st	125.00
WC Furniture - 28th	25.00
NCS Visa - 2nd	80.00
Student loan - 1st	50.00
Car loan - 15th	<u>182.32</u>
(car loan was divided)	
Total	$892.32

Remaining misc. $78.08
(Includes amount for groceries and
other miscellaneous expenses)

75

It is important not to list a bill under a paycheck that will cause that bill to be late. Since you will be using the due dates to your advantage, you may actually collect the money in your checking account for a bill before you receive that bill in the mail.

For example, let's say you have a bill that is normally due on the fifth day of every month. However, you also have three other bills that are due between the first and third day of each month. You receive paychecks on the first and the fifteenth day of each month. Let's assume that if you paid all four bills from one paycheck, you would not have money left for food. You would definitely have a problem. But if you list the bill that is due on the fifth under your first paycheck of the month and the other three bills under the second paycheck, all of the bills are paid without any hardship. In this example, you are actually collecting the money for the three bills almost three weeks before they are due. See figure 6-4.

Fig. 6-4 Another Example of Equal Distribution

First Paycheck dte rcvd - 1st	$750.00	
Rent - 1st	204.50	
Car loan/ins -1st	**282.50**	←
Gas & Elec -10th	120.00	
Cable - 15th	36.00	
BB Visa - 5th	**50.00**	←
Remaining Misc	$57.00	

Second Paycheck dte rcvd - 15th	$750.00	
Rent 1st	204.50	
Car loan/ins- 1st	**282.50**	←
Sec Pac MC - 3rd	**80.00**	←
CM Visa - 1st	**50.00**	←
Telephone - 2nd	**80.00**	←
Remaining Misc	$53.00	

At first, it may seem difficult to collect the money well in advance of due dates, but if you force it you can make it work. Also, as with your mortgage or rent, there may be other bills that you may want to divide by the number of paychecks you receive each month. By dividing certain larger bills you will evenly distribute your monthly expenses. For example, you have a car payment of $565 per month. If you divide this bill by 2, you will be setting aside $282.50 from each paycheck for your car loan. See Figure 6-4. I found it less of a financial burden to distribute certain larger bills in this manner.

If it is to your advantage to divide some of your other larger bills, just as you did with the rent or mortgage, don't forget to list those bills under each paycheck on your worksheet.

5. Is that all I have left?

Now that you have evenly distributed your bills based on due dates and the dates you receive each paycheck, exactly how much do you have left per paycheck after all obligations are deducted? This remaining amount is what you have left for miscellaneous spending. This amount would also include groceries if you did not include groceries as part of your expenses under each paycheck. For the sample payment schedule, I purposely did not include groceries as an actual expense under the paychecks. This was done because it is up to you whether you want to buy a set amount of groceries each week or whether you want to spend a certain amount of your grocery money eating out.

THE PROCESS OF GETTING OUT OF DEBT

When I was going through the process of getting out of debt, I included "Groceries" in the expenses section under each paycheck, but this is a personal preference.

The remaining miscellaneous amount is sometimes an eye opener. The common question is, "Is that all I have left?" Unfortunately most of the time the answer is yes.

If this is the first time you have actually developed a payment schedule for your monthly financial obligations, you may not be able to believe what you are seeing. In the past whenever payday rolled around, you would go out and buy stuff. Yes, you had bills to pay, but you also wanted to spend some of your hard earned cash. Little did you know you shouldn't have been spending any more than the miscellaneous amount you have just discovered. This miscellaneous amount also includes any amount you would like to save which I will discuss later.

The miscellaneous amount includes any expenditure that is not listed as a regular bill on your "Monthly Payment Schedule." Regardless of the actual amount of your paycheck, this remaining miscellaneous amount is all you have to work with. The rest of the money is already accounted for. In order to ensure you do not tap into your obligated funds, you want to keep a running balance of your remaining miscellaneous amount. A good way to keep track of the miscellaneous amount is to maintain a ledger. The ledger is very similar to your checkbook ledger; however, your miscellaneous ledger will only include the balance of your remaining

DROWNING IN DEBT? GET OUT AND STAY OUT!

miscellaneous amount.

Let's take another look at the examples in Figures 6-2 and 6-3. You will notice that every expense with a check mark, is also listed under one of the paychecks. Notice that the remaining miscellaneous amount for the first paycheck is $97.08. The remaining amount under the second check is $78.08. The total remaining miscellaneous amount for this sample month is $175.16.

But what is the total amount of the expenses without check marks on the sample "Monthly Expenses Worksheet"? The total is $688. If this example represented a picture of your financial situation for the month, you would be spending $512.84 above and beyond what you are actually earning. At this rate, you would never get out of debt. In fact you would sink deeper and deeper into debt. This is precisely why you want to keep a ledger of the amount available for miscellaneous expenses.

The "Remaining Miscellaneous Ledger" is a compliment to the "Payment Schedule." See Figure 6-5 for an example. In this example, the first amount listed under the "Jan" column is $97.08 which would represent the current balance of the miscellaneous amount. When you add to or withdraw from the miscellaneous amount, you will indicate the "date" followed by a "/", a "+" or "-" and then the amount. You would then reflect the new balance in the "Bal" column. So, in the example in figure 6-5, you can see that on Jan 2, $20 was withdrawn. The new balance of $77.08 is reflected directly under that entry. The next

THE PROCESS OF GETTING OUT OF DEBT

entry reflects a $40 withdrawal on Jan 6, leaving a balance of $37.08. As you can see on Jan 15, $78.08 was added.

Whatever you have left over at the end of any given month is simply carried over as the beginning balance to the next month. A blank Miscellaneous Ledger is included at the end of step six for your use.

Figure 6-5 Sample Miscellaneous Ledger

	Jan	Feb	Mar	Apr	May
Bal	97.08	20	41.71	45.77	47.79
+/-	2/-20	1/+95.88	1/+106.58	1/+99.94	1/+104.33
Bal	77.08	115.88	148.29	145.71	152.12
+/-	6/-40	3/-60	4/-40	2/-45	3/-50
Bal	37.08	55.88	108.29	100.71	102.12
+/-	11/-10	10/-20	8/-20	9/30	11/-20
Bal	27.08	35.88	88.29	70.71	82.12
+/-	15/+78.08	15/+75.83	13/-20	15/+69.08	15/+79.58
Bal	105.16	111.71	68.29	139.79	161.70
+/-	17/-25.16	16/-40	15/+72.48	18/-60	17/-50
Bal	80	71.71	140.77	79.79	111.70
+/-	22/-40	21/-20	18/-50	20/-15	22/-30
Bal	40	51.71	90.77	64.79	81.70
+/-	28/-20	28/-10	24/-30	29/-17	
Bal	20	41.71	60.77	47.79	
+/-			29/-15		
Bal			45.77		
+/-					
Bal					
+/-					
Bal					
+/-					
Bal					

6. Pay-off projection dates

Pay-off projection dates are for your benefit only. The pay-off projection dates served as an incentive while paying off my credit cards and student loans. Essentially, I knew exactly when the last payment would be paid. You will have weak moments, but when you pick up your "Monthly Payment Schedule" and see how close you are to that first, second, third or even last pay-off date, you have an incentive to keep going.

You will need an incentive because after a couple of months, you are actually paying money the credit card companies are not requesting. It can be really tempting to take that extra amount and use it for something else. Just keep reminding yourself how nice it will be when you make that last payment with interest. Remember when you pay interest, you are paying some company or bank for the privilege of buying stuff. Hopefully, the mere thought of this fact will be an incentive to continue paying the increased monthly payment amounts.

I can say that since I finished paying off that last credit card, I have never carried a credit card balance over to the next month. If I charge it that month, I pay it that month. It has become a habit. If you add up all of your monthly credit card and loan payments, the amount is probably pretty substantial. Eventually, that is how much you will have at your disposal to spend any way you please. To add to your disposable income, you may even pick up a few salary increases along the way. So don't give up.

THE PROCESS OF GETTING OUT OF DEBT

It is not necessary to calculate down to the penny when determining your pay-off dates. As I said earlier, this is for your benefit only. To keep my promise that there is no need to be an accountant or financial wizard to follow this book, I am going to keep things simple. Granted, there are computer programs out there that can calculate what day and hour you will pay off each of your accounts, and if you have one of those programs, feel free to use it. But it is not necessary to go out and purchase one of these programs just to calculate your pay-off dates.

To determine your pay-off dates the old fashion way, start with the lowest balance again. I will continue to use the sample "Monthly Expenses Worksheet" for illustration purposes. The lowest balance on the sample worksheet is a student loan for $650, and the payments are set at $50 per month. $650 divided by 50 is 13 months. The interest rates on student loans are normally very low so I would add an additional month to account for the interest. Therefore, the pay-off date for the student loan would be 14 months from today.

This may seem like forever for such a small balance, but after you finish the first few balances, things will speed up. And your personal situation may allow you to significantly increase your monthly payments. For the purpose of this exercise, let's assume we started the process of getting out of debt in January 1997, a New Year's resolution. So the pay-off date for the student loan would be reflected on the payment schedule as follows:

Pay-off Feb 98
Student loan - 1st $50

    Continuing with this example, you know when the first balance will be paid in full. Now you need to determine the next pay-off date. Your next lowest balance is $800 and the minimum payment for this account is $25, which you will continue to pay during the time frame the student loan is being paid off. As we have determined, the student loan will be paid off in 14 months. Now multiply $25 X 14 months = $350.

    During the 14 month period, $350 is the amount that will be paid toward the $800 balance, part of which is interest. Let's assume the interest on this account is 14%. I would take the $800 balance that we started with and determine that 14% of that amount is $112. I realize the actual interest for this account would be less than the $112 because of the reduction of the $800 beginning balance.

    I subtracted the interest based on the full 14% of the original amount for a couple of reasons. First, we are dealing with a full year's time frame. Second, there is future interest to take into account. In fact, when you are calculating the pay-off dates for accounts that are two years or more from the day you start getting out of debt, you should subtract a full 1.5 year of interest from the amount of the total payments made, in order to determine the new starting balance. You would then divide your new balance by the new enhanced monthly payment to

THE PROCESS OF GETTING OUT OF DEBT

determine the number of months until that account is paid in full. This would be your pay-off date. If your pay-off date includes a fraction of a month up to 1/2 of a month, round up to the next month. If the fraction exceeds 1/2 of a month, you should round up to the next month and then add an additional month to the pay-off date.

My personal experience was that the pay-off dates were accurate within one month using this formula. Remember, the pay-off dates are for your benefit only so you do not have to spend forever figuring them out to the day, unless you want to, of course.

Continuing with this example, take the $350 that was paid during the 14-month time frame and subtract the $112 in interest; you have $238. Now subtract $238 from $800 which is $562 for the new balance. Your new payment for this account will be $75 instead of $25 because the $50 payment previously used to pay off the student loan will be added. Now take the $562 and divide it by $75 = 7.5 months, rounded up to eight months. The pay-off date for the $800 balance is October 1998, eight months beyond the February 1998 pay-off date for the student loan.

You would start determining the next pay-off date by multiplying the amount of the set monthly payment for that account times 22 months. 22 months is obtained by adding the 14 months for the student loan account to the eight months for the $800 account. Continue by following the above instructions. See figure 6-6.

85

Figure 6-6
Credit Accounts with Pay-off Dates

First paycheck - 1st	$970.40
Rent - 1st	350.00
Water & Sewer - 15th	65.00
Cable - 15th	56.00
HC Dept Store - 10th (Pay-off Apr 99)	30.00
Sec Pac MC - 3rd (Pay-off Sep 99)	50.00
Telephone - 22nd	80.00
CM Visa - 18th (Pay-off Dec 99)	60.00
Car loan - 15th (Pay-off Nov 99)	182.32
Total	873.32
Remaining misc.	97.08

Second Paycheck - 15th	$970.40
Rent - 1st	350.00
Gas & Electric - 17th	80.00
Car insurance - 1st	125.00
WC Furniture - 28th (Pay-off Oct 98)	25.00
NCS Visa - 2nd (Pay-off Jan 2000)	80.00
Student loan - 1st (Pay-off Feb 98)	50.00
Car loan - 15th (pay-off Nov 99)	182.32
Total	892.32
Remaining misc.	78.08

7. Don't get discouraged

Don't get discouraged by the amount of time it takes to become debt-free. It simply takes longer to pay off credit account balances than it does to accumulate them. As time passes, you may be able to add to the amount you are paying on your lowest balances because of raises or bonuses. In the above example of the second balance, it would have taken in excess of 32 months instead of 22 months to finish paying the $800 balance, had the minimum payment not been increased. If you do receive raises or bonuses, I suggest adding at least a portion of those amounts to the lowest balance.

8. Putting it all together

You have determined the minimum amount you will consistently pay on each bill and you have arranged the monthly due dates to your advantage. You know how much you have to work with after expenses and how to keep track of what you are spending from your miscellaneous pool of funds. You have also determined when each account will be paid in full. Now you want to keep track of all of this information. To do that we will transfer everything to the final payment schedule.
You will maintain your payment schedule throughout the entire process of getting out of debt, updating it on a regular basis. At a glance,

you will be able to pick up your payment schedule and observe your progress. If you find yourself falling off track, just get back on schedule and continue. It is best to file your payment schedule wherever you will keep your monthly account statements. Figures 6-7 through 6-22 show the sample debts starting at day-one of the process of getting out of debt through payment in full.

Figure 6-7 Sample Payment Schedule

First Paycheck	Jan	1997 Feb	Mar	Apr
Dte Rcvd - 1st	970.40	970.40	970.40	970.40
Rent - 1st	350	350	350	350
Wtr & Swr - 15th	65	62	56	60
Cable - 15th	56	56	56	56
Pay-off Apr 99 HC Dept St - 10th	30	30	30	30
Pay-off Sep 99 Sec Pac MC - 3rd	50	50	50	50
Telephone - 22nd	80	84.20	79.50	82.14
Pay-off Dec 99 CM Visa - 18th	60	60	60	60
Pay-off Nov 99 Car loan - 15th	182.32	182.32	182.32	182.32
TOTAL Expenses	873.32	874.52	863.82	870.46
Remaining Misc	97.08	95.88	106.58	99.94

In this example, very little is left after all expenses are accounted for. As a result, the use of the remaining amount must be carefully tracked by using a miscellaneous ledger.

Figure 6-8 Sample Payment Schedule

First Paycheck cont.			1997		
May	Jun	July	Aug	Sep	Oct
970.40	995.50	995.50	995.50	995.50	995.50
350	350	350	350	350	350
62.25	65	69.50	71	68.90	72.50
56	56	56	56	56	56
30	30	30	30	30	30
50	50	50	50	50	50
75.50	88.20	85	67.19	84.50	39.15
60	60	60	60	60	60
182.32	182.32	182.32	182.32	182.32	182.32
866.07	881.52	882.82	866.51	881.72	839.97
104.33	113.98	112.68	128.99	113.78	155.53

Figure 6-9 Sample Payment Schedule

Second Paycheck	1997			
	Jan	Feb	Mar	Apr
Dte Rcvd - 15th	970.40	970.40	970.40	970.40
Rent - 1st	350	350	350	350
Gas & Elec - 17th	80	82.25	85.60	89
Car Ins - 1st	125	125	125	125
Pay-off Oct 98 WC Furni - 28th	25	25	25	25
Pay-off Jan 2000 NCS Visa - 2nd	80	80	80	80
Pay-off Feb 98 Student loan - 1st	50	50	50	50
Pay-off Nov 99 Car loan - 15th	182.32	182.32	182.32	182.32
TOTAL Expenses	892.32	895.08	897.92	901.32
Remaining Misc	78.08	75.32	72.48	69.08

The remaining miscellaneous amount is what is left over after other expenses are deducted.

Figure 6-10 Sample Payment Schedule

Second Paycheck cont			1997		
May	Jun	July	Aug	Sep	Oct
970.40	995.50	995.50	995.50	995.50	995.50
350	350	350	350	350	350
78.50	84.60	80.15	81.14	86	85.60
125	125	125	125	125	125
25	25	25	25	25	25
80	80	80	80	80	80
50	50	50	50	50	50
182.32	182.32	182.32	182.32	182.32	182.32
890.82	896.92	892.47	893.46	898.32	897.92
79.58	98.58	103.03	102.04	97.18	97.58

Figure 6-11 Sample Payment Schedule

First check cont	1997 Nov	Dec	1998 Jan	Feb
Dte Rcvd - 1st	995.50	995.50	995.50	995.50
Rent - 1st	350	350	350	350
Wtr & Swr - 15th	56.80	62.19	61	68.40
Cable - 15th	56	56	56	56
Pay-off Apr 99 HC Dept St - 10th	30	30	30	30
Pay-off Sep 99 Sec Pac MC - 3rd	50	50	50	50
Telephone - 22nd	40	61.25	68.50	64.14
Pay-off Dec 99 CM Visa - 18th	60	60	60	60
Pay-off Nov 99 Car loan - 15th	182.32	182.32	182.32	182.32
TOTAL Expenses	825.12	851.76	857.82	860.86
Remaining Misc	170.38	143.74	137.68	134.64

Notice that the telephone bill has been consistantly lower over the last several months which in turn, has increased the "Remaining Misc" amount.

Figure 6-12 Sample Payment Schedule

First Paycheck cont.			1998		
Mar	Apr	May	Jun	Jul	Aug
995.50	995.50	995.50	995.50	995.50	995.50
350	350	350	350	350	350
60.25	65.80	69	61.20	68	72.50
56	56	56	56	56	56
30	30	30	30	30	30
50	50	50	50	50	50
55.50	68.20	56.60	57.19	44.50	39.15
60	60	60	60	60	60
182.32	182.32	182.32	182.32	182.32	182.32
844.07	862.32	853.92	846.71	840.82	839.97
151.43	133.18	141.58	148.79	154.68	155.53

DROWNING IN DEBT? GET OUT AND STAY OUT!

Figure 6-13 Sample Payment Schedule

Second Paycheck cont	1997		1998	
	Nov	Dec	Jan	Feb
Dte Rcvd - 15th	995.50	995.50	995.50	995.50
Rent - 1st	350	350	350	350
Gas & Elec - 17th	81.60	84.32	79.40	78.14
Car Ins - 1st	125	125	125	125
Pay-off Oct 98 WC Furni - 28th	25	25	25	25
Pay-off Jan 2000 NCS Visa - 2nd	80	80	80	80
Pay-off Feb 98 Student loan - 1st	50	50	50	→ 50
Pay-off Nov 99 Car loan - 15th	182.32	182.32	182.32	182.32
TOTAL Expenses	893.92	896.64	891.72	890.46
Remaining Misc →	101.58	98.86	103.78	105.04

As your income increases or extra income is obtained, the miscellaneous amount will increase.

Last payment for student loan.

96

THE PROCESS OF GETTING OUT OF DEBT

Figure 6-14 Sample Payment Schedule

Second Paycheck cont			1998		
Mar	Apr	May	Jun	Jul	Aug
995.50	995.50	995.50	995.50	995.50	995.50
350	350	350	350	350	350
81.50	85.66	78..15	79.22	81.40	80.21
125 75 25	125 75 25	125 75 25	125 75 25	125 75 25	125 75 25
80 ~~50~~	80 ~~50~~	80 ~~50~~	80 ~~50~~	80 ~~50~~	80 ~~50~~
182.32	182.32	182.32	182.32	182.32	182.32
893.82	897.98	890.47	891.54	893.72	892.53
101.68	97.52	105.03	103.96	101.78	102.97

Wc Furniture payment is now $75.
Payment consists of: Stdnt ln $50
           WC Fur $25
           Total $75

After an account has been paid in full, simply "X" out the box but continue to calculate that amount untill all other credit accounts are paid in full.

97

DROWNING IN DEBT? GET OUT AND STAY OUT!

Figure 6-15 Sample Payment Schedule

| First check cont | 1998 | | | |
	Sep	Oct	Nov	Dec
Dte Rcvd - 1st	995.50	995.50	995.50	995.50
Rent - 1st	350	350	350	350
Wtr & Swr - 15th	52.20	55.59	59.20	56.40
Cable - 15th	56	56	56	56
Pay-off Apr 99			105	105
HC Dept St - 10th	30	30	30	30
Pay-off Sep 99				
Sec Pac MC - 3rd	50	50	50	50
Telephone - 22nd	50.65	45.55	59.46	62.24
Pay-off Dec 99				
CM Visa - 18th	60	60	60	60
Pay-off Nov 99				
Car loan - 15th	182.32	182.32	182.32	182.32
TOTAL Expenses	831.17	829.46	846.98	846.96
Remaining Misc	164.33	166.04	148.52	148.54

Note $105 is now the payment for HC Dept. The payment consists of: Stdt loan $50
WC Furn $25
HC Dept $30
$105

Continue to use $30 to calculate expenses under the first check (**Not** $105).

98

THE PROCESS OF GETTING OUT OF DEBT

Figure 6-16 Sample Payment Schedule

First Paycheck cont.			1999		
Jan	Feb	Mar	Apr	May	Jun
995.50	1015.41	1015.41	1015.41	1015.41	1015.41
350	350	350	350	350	350
61.65	68.50	71.02	59.99	61.11	72.56
56	56	56	56	56	56
105	105	105	105		
30	30	30	30	~~30~~	~~30~~
				155	155
50	50	50	50	50	50
58.50	56.21	51.60	67.25	64.10	49.50
60	60	60	60	60	60
182.32	182.32	182.32	182.32	182.32	182.32
848.47	853.03	850.94	855.56	853.53	850.38
168.94	162.38	164.47	159.85	161.88	165.03

New Payment for Sec Pac Mc is $155. Payment now consists of:
 Stdt loan $50
 WC Furn $25
 HC Dept $30
 Sec Pac MC $50
            $155

Continue to use the original payment for calculation purposes even after the final payment is made--Simply X out the box but continue to show payment amount.

99

DROWNING IN DEBT? GET OUT AND STAY OUT!

Figure 6-17 Sample Payment Schedule

Second Paycheck cont	1998			
	Sep	Oct	Nov	Dec
Dte Rcvd - 15th	995.50	995.50	995.50	995.50
Rent - 1st	350	350	350	350
Gas & Elec - 17th	83.55	82.44	80.40	79.99
Car Ins - 1st	125	125	125	125
Pay-off Oct 98 WC Furni - 28th	75 / 25	75 / 25	~~25~~	~~25~~
Pay-off Jan 2000 NCS Visa - 2nd	80	80	80	80
Pay-off Feb 98 Student loan - 1st	~~50~~	~~50~~	~~50~~	~~50~~
Pay-off Nov 99 Car loan - 15th	182.32	182.32	182.32	182.32
TOTAL Expenses	895.87	894.76	892.72	892.31
Remaining Misc	99.63	100.74	102.78	103.19

List the actual payment in the top left corner of the box but use the original payment amount (**Not the actual payment**) to calculate expenses.

100

THE PROCESS OF GETTING OUT OF DEBT

Figure 6-18 Sample Payment Schedule

Second Paycheck cont			1999		
Jan	Feb	Mar	Apr	May	Jun
995.50	1015.41	1015.41	1015.41	1015.41	1015.41
350	350	350	350	350	350
78.44	81.01	79.25	83.22	77.60	80.33
125	125	125	125	125	125
~~25~~	~~25~~	~~25~~	~~25~~	~~25~~	~~25~~
80	80	80	80	80	80
~~50~~	~~50~~	~~50~~	~~50~~	~~50~~	~~50~~
182.32	182.32	182.32	182.32	182.32	182.32
890.76	893.33	891.57	895.54	889.92	892.65
124.65	122.08	123.84	119.87	125.49	122.76

101

DROWNING IN DEBT? GET OUT AND STAY OUT!

Figure 6-19 Sample Payment Schedule

| First check cont | 1999 | | | |
	Jul	Aug	Sep	Oct
Dte Rcvd - 1st	1015.41	1015.41	1015.41	1015.41
Rent - 1st	350	350	350	350
Wtr & Swr - 15th	62.25	45.49	63.20	66.44
Cable - 15th	56	56	56	56
Pay-off Apr 99				
HC Dept St - 10th	~~30~~	~~30~~	~~30~~	~~30~~
Pay-off Sep 99	155	155	155	
Sec Pac MC - 3rd	50	50	50	~~50~~
Telephone - 22nd	58.90	32.32	49.80	72.50
Pay-off Dec 99				215
CM Visa - 18th	60	60	60	60
Pay-off Nov 99				
Car loan - 15th	182.32	182.32	182.32	182.32
TOTAL Expenses	849.47	806.13	841.32	867.26
Remaining Misc	165.94	209.28	174.09	148.15

CM Visa payment is now $215. The
payment consists of:

    Stdt loan $50
    WC Furn $25
    HC Dept $30
    Sec Pac MC $50
    CM Visa $60
                            $215

THE PROCESS OF GETTING OUT OF DEBT

Figure 6-20 Sample Payment Schedule

First check	1999		2000			
Nov	Dec	Jan	Feb	Mar	Apr
1015.41	1015.41	1015.41	1015.41	1015.41	1015.41
350	350	350	350	350	350
63.35	58.80	75.55	69.77	61	70.26
56	56	56	56	56	56
~~30~~	~~30~~	~~30~~			
~~50~~	~~50~~	~~50~~			
44.44	39.99	60.28	55.60	52.62	70.30
215	579.64				
60	60	~~60~~			
182.32	~~182.32~~	~~182.32~~			
836.11	827.11	864.15	531.37	519.62	546.56
179.30	188.30	151.26	484.04	495.79	468.85

Last payment for CM Visa also includes amount for car loan. The last payment should actually be less than $579.64.

Remember, the last scheduled bill to be paid in full was NCS Visa in January 2000. Once the last bill is finished, there is no need to continue calculating the other credit accounts as part of the monthly expenses.

103

Figure 6-21 Sample Payment Schedule

Second Paycheck cont	1999			
	Jul	Aug	Sep	Oct
Dte Rcvd - 15th	1015.41	1015.41	1015.41	1015.41
Rent - 1st	350	350	350	350
Gas & Elec - 17th	77.78	83.53	79.55	78.40
Car Ins - 1st	125	125	125	125
Pay-off Oct 98 WC Furni - 28th	~~25~~	~~25~~	~~25~~	~~25~~
Pay-off Jan 2000 NCS Visa - 2nd	80	80	80	80
Pay-off Feb 98 Student loan - 1st	~~50~~	~~50~~	~~50~~	~~50~~
Pay-off Nov 99 Car loan - 15th	182.32	182.32	182.32	182.32
TOTAL Expenses	890.10	895.85	891.87	890.72
Remaining Misc	125.31	119.56	123.54	124.69

Figure 6-22 Sample Payment Schedule

2nd ck cont 1999 Nov	Dec	Jan	2000 Feb	Mar	Apr
1015.41	1015.41	1015.41	1015.41	1015.41	1015.41
350	350	350	350	350	350
81.11	83.82	77.30	79.34	77.50	70.34
125	125	125	125	125	125
~~25~~	~~25~~	~~25~~			
~~80~~	~~80~~	659.64 ▲ 80			
~~50~~	~~50~~	~~50~~			
~~182.32~~	~~182.32~~	~~182.32~~			
893.43	896.14	889.62	554.34	552.50	545.34
121.98	119.27	125.79	461.07	462.91	470.07

Last month for car payment.

Final payment for all credit accounts.

NCS Visa payment now consists of::
Stdt ln $50
WC Furn $25
HC Dpt $30
Sec Pac MC $50
CM Visa $60
Car Loan $364.64
NCS Visa $80
Total $659.64

Figure 6-23 Blank Payment Schedule

First Paycheck				
Dte Rcvd -				

THE PROCESS OF GETTING OUT OF DEBT

Figure 6-24 Blank Payment Schedule

First Paycheck cont					

Figure 6-25 Blank Payment Schedule

Second Paycheck Dte Rcvd -				

Figure 6-26 Blank Payment Schedule

Second Paycheck cont					

Figure 6-27 Blank Miscellaneous Cash Ledger

Bal					
+/-					
Bal					
+/-					
Bal					
+/-					
Bal					
+/-					
Bal					
+/-					
Bal					
+/-					
Bal					
+/-					
Bal					
+/-					
Bal					
+/-					
Bal					
+/-					
Bal					

Seventh Step

Staying out of debt!

D ebt is so easy to get into, but it is very difficult and often painful to get out of debt. If you are not careful, continuing to stay out of debt can be even more difficult. One of my goals for this book is to help people change the attitudes and behaviors that resulted in their being in debt in the first place. Before reading this book, maybe you believed being in debt had everything to do with a lack of money. Maybe you thought, "If only I had more money, I would not be in this situation." Hopefully, you now realize that is not necessarily true.

Earlier, I gave a scenario about two individuals who began to experience financial difficulties around the same time and they were each given $50,000 to start over again. The one who was able to wisely manage the money was the one who benefited from the generous gift. The other individual continued to have financial problems. The purpose of that example was to show it is not always a matter of how much you have, but how well you manage what you have. That is the key to staying out of debt.

1. "Don't buy it if you can't pay for it"

This is a quote from my Grandmother and a motto she lives by. For a person with no formal training in financial management, she has a very unique and sound financial perspective. By no means does she have a lot of money, but she manages what she does have very well. I don't think I have ever met anyone who can stretch a dollar as far as Grandma does.

We can all learn from Grandma's motto. Some of us in the credit card generation may say, "I can pay for it with my credit card," but where has that kind of thinking gotten us? It has gotten us in debt. So staying out of debt may require us to do things the old fashioned way and save for it. What a radical idea! Once you have paid off all your credit card accounts, saving for purchases shouldn't be a problem.

Saving for large purchases offers several benefits. One benefit is you are not creating new debt. Another benefit is you have a chance to "cool off." You may later find that you really didn't want or need a certain item after all. However, if you have a habit of making credit card purchases on the spur of the moment, you may find yourself regretting it later. This could be true especially when it may take years to pay for the purchase. By saving for large purchases, you also eliminate the need to pay interest.

Work toward changing your mode of operating. Adopt a policy that says, "I'm not going to make any purchase over a certain dollar value before I have had at least one day, maybe two days, to think about it." Make the dollar value a relatively small amount. Remember the small dollar purchases can be just as damaging as the large purchases. Sales representatives have a hard time with people who think before they purchase. They know if you walk away you may not come back. When you walk away, you are taking control of your impulse to spend.

Just think about this as an example. There may be a time when you are out at the mall just window shopping. You really don't have any intention of buying anything, but there in front of you someone is selling a food dehydrator. You have never had one; in fact you have never known anyone who owns one. You listen for awhile and for some reason you start to think, "I think I need one of these things and besides, its not that expensive." The sales person has done exactly what he or she is being paid to do--get people to think they simply must have a food dehydrator. If you thought about it overnight, would the food dehydrator be the first thing on your mind the next day? More than likely not.

I used a food dehydrator to illustrate my point. It could just as well have been a car, furniture, hardware, electronics, clothing, etc.

Wherever you are, give yourself some time to think before making a purchase.

One of the best things you can do is to start planning for large purchases months or even years before you would like to make the purchase. You also want to plan for the unforeseen events that always pop-up, but are never planned. I know a couple who is saving now for a sailboat they do not plan to purchase for several years in the future. They are actually saving for the boat by depositing money into an aggressive growth mutual fund account. They refer to this account as their "toy fund." They deposit any "windfall" or extra money into this account. A portion of a tax refund, a property tax reduction, a rebate, or any unexpected money is what this couple refers to as "windfall" money.

This same couple also developed separate accounts earmarked for both their cars. They make car payments into two separate "car funds" even though they never actually make car payments to a bank or dealership. By doing this, they never pay any interest when purchasing a vehicle because they are paying in cash. Instead, they are gaining interest because they are saving within a mutual fund. The other benefit is the car payments they are paying into the mutual funds are relatively low because they are always making the payments. If the funds become larger than what they need to buy their desired vehicles, they simply transfer the money into one of their other funds. This couple saves for their children's college education using the same principles. Essentially, their financial management is the antithesis of drowning in debt. Adopting their methods would be a plus for any household.

When saving in advance for miscellaneous mishaps or larger purchases, it is not necessary to save using separate mutual fund accounts. Although, by doing so, you may be able to gain a considerable amount of interest on your money. You can save for large purchases and other expenses by using your regular savings and checking accounts if you desire. In principle, you want to separate your special savings amounts from your day-to-day living expense amounts even though it is all in the same account. You can do this by using a separate ledger that is similar to your miscellaneous spending ledger. Just simply designate the various items you are saving for on a sheet of paper. You then keep track of the deposits you have earmarked for the specific items. See figure 7-1 as an example.

Figure 7-1 Sample Savings Ledger

Household Repairs			Medical expenses		
Bal		$460	Bal		$1,100
3/6	+	$50	2/15	+	$90
Bal		$510	Bal		$1,190

Entertainment			Large Screen TV		
Bal		$75	Bal		$350
2/28	+	$15	4/1	+	$150
Bal		$90	Bal		$500

Car Repairs		
Bal		$460
3/20	-	$220
Bal		$240

2. What about your new popularity?

Once you have paid off a couple of your accounts, you will be more popular than you know. Your name will be popping up on new mailing lists all around the country. As a result, you will start receiving even more pre-approved offers to accept new credit cards and loans. Some of these offers will claim to have unbelievably low interest rates and other wonderful benefits. What are you going to do? I personally do not read any of those offers. Some people do and they, in turn, may find some excellent deals.

In addition to unrelated credit card offers, you may even receive an offer with blank checks from one of your current credit card companies. In principle, all you need to do is sign and use the checks. Often times there is very confusing language that accompany these checks. What you may not understand is that any balance generated as a result of using these checks is separate from your actual credit card balance. Until the check balance is paid in full, the primary balance is held in abeyance while accruing interest. Who benefits from that? The lender, of course.

As with making purchases, do not allow any of these credit card and loan offers to make a decision for you. If you are shopping around for better interest rates, shop wisely and read the fine print. On the other hand, if you know you have a weakness in the area of credit cards, avoid these offers, just don't look at them. Its just that simple.

3. What's next?

When your credit accounts are all paid in full, what is your next goal? Well, that all depends on you and your personal circumstance. Do you have school age children? Do you have a mortgage? Will you be retiring in the not-so-distant future? Would you like to start an investment plan? When you don't have a slew of credit card bills hanging over your head, you are able to give these questions some serious consideration. Not only are you able to give these questions consideration, you are actually free to implement a plan.

Investment plan for Children - If you have dependent children, what steps can you take financially to help them prepare for their future. An important step you can take is to stress the consequences of being in debt by using yourself as an example. Another step is to start an investment college fund for your children. There are a number of different options from which to choose. Some options are more risky than others. Of course, one of the safest options is a savings account. Normally, the return on a regular savings account is not very much. Another safe option is the age-old U.S. savings bonds. U.S. savings bonds are very safe and the returns are very predictable. Normally, there is a $25 minimum deposit and the bonds mature in 7 to 10 years. Some bonds such as EE bonds, as well as many other types of bonds, have tax advantages. If you have very young children, savings bonds as well as a number of other types of bonds may be good possibilities.

Another option for your children is to establish a trust. Once established, any type of asset may be used to fund the trust. CDs, real property, and mutual funds are just three examples of some of the things that could be placed in a trust. Some trusts are irrevocable. Once you set up an irrevocable trust you cannot make any changes. No one wants to think this way, but the child may be involved in something at age 18 or 21 that you may not want to condone or support by having several thousand dollars at his or her disposal--just something to consider. The child/beneficiary will receive the proceeds of the trust as specified by the grantor. This is a very complicated area of the law which requires the assistance of an attorney who specializes in this area.

There are many other options to consider as investment possibilities for your children. Check your Yellow Pages under investments or check with co-workers and friends to obtain personal references. You should be able to set up a meeting with a broker, free of charge, to discuss the many options available to you.

Paying-off the mortgage early - Most people think of their mortgage as something that will always be around, but there is a way to pay it off years early. Without credit card bills, you will be able to take advantage of this possibility. Let's assume your mortgage is $1,000 per month, a nice round figure. When you first start paying on your mortgage, most of the monthly payment is earmarked for interest. It is possible that more than $900 of this $1,000 payment will be applied to interest with no more than $100 going toward the principal balance. But, if you paid an additional $500 towards the principal, essentially you would be paying the equivalent of an additional 5 months in mortgage payments.

The same was true with your credit card bills. The more you paid above the amount due, the more you reduced the principal balance. If you paid a couple of extra mortgage payments each year, you would be reducing your principal balance by years. Contact your mortgage company for more information about applying additional payments to your principal balance. Of course, if you are renting, but would like to purchase a home, use this same philosophy to save for the down payment.

Planning for retirement - Today, it is fairly easy to take an active role in planning for your retirement. Most companies and government agencies offer some type of investment retirement plan that will match a set percentage of your contributions. This type of retirement plan is most commonly referred to as a "401K" account. Most experts will recommend that you take maximum advantage of any plan when an employer is matching a portion of your contributions. In most cases, your actual contributions and earnings are tax deferred. You do not pay taxes until you start withdrawing the money, which in most cases will be at a lower tax rate than your current rate. Of course, a 401K plan is in addition to your regular Social Security retirement. Today, most of us are not feeling very secure about our Social Security retirement benefits, which is why additional retirement planning is so important.

In addition to a 401K and Social Security, you also can take measures to supplement your retirement with an Individual Retirement Account (IRA). In some cases, an IRA may be the only retirement an individual has. The rules on IRAs have changed over the years. At one time, you could deduct income taxes based on your IRA contributions regardless of your income. Now however, if you make over $50,000 as a couple or over $35,000 as a single person, you get no tax break for IRA contributions. Below those respective incomes, you can receive a tax break up to $2,000. This applies only if you are not an active participant in a retirement plan at work. But if you're not an active participant at work or if you're self employed, the $2,000 tax deduction applies regardless of your income.

There is no need to be a miser regarding your retirement, but you should have some plan in place that you have carefully thought about. You don't want to deliberately plan to depend on others to support you during your retirement years. Of course, uncontrollable circumstances could put you in that position, but it certainly should not be part of your planning or lack of planning.

Investment plan in general - Have you always been curious about investing in general, but just didn't know how to get started? Maybe you believed you needed a truck load of cash to get started. Well, its not a very complicated process and the amount to invest is your decision. As with starting an investment plan for your children or planning for your own retirement, a financial broker will be able to assist you with any general investing you would like to do.

If you would like to become more familiar with what's out there for investment possibilities, start reading the business section of your local newspaper. If your paper does not have a business section or if it is very limited, the New York Times, Wall Street Journal, or the USA Today newspapers are very good sources. Your goal is to obtain information about any new innovative products and ideas in the business community that may be good investment possibilities. Your local public library is also an excellent source to learn more about a company you may find interesting.

Investing is like anything else in life. Once you become familiar with the "dos" and the "don'ts," and the terminology, it becomes second nature.

What about charitable contributions? The act of giving is a very personal thing. The reasons for giving or not giving are numerous. Some of us give as a result of our love and appreciation for our Lord Jesus Christ. There are some who give out of a sense of duty to others less fortunate than they are, while some will say it is not their duty to support others. And some give to receive a tax advantage. Not only are there numerous reasons for giving or not giving, there are emotions behind those reasons as well.

I wanted to briefly touch on this topic in hope that you may give it some consideration in your day-to-day activities. I am a firm believer in helping people learn and understand how to help themselves. The act of giving does not necessarily mean giving money. There is time, expertise, companionship and a number of other resources you may possess or have access to.

There is also no magical dollar amount or number of hours that must be committed to helping others. So give it some thought.

4. A final note

I certainly hope the information you have read in this book will prove to be a valuable tool in your quest to become debt-free. I commend you for making the decision to address your debt situation. Far too many people make the decision to do nothing. When a decision is made to do nothing, the rest of us bear the extra burden in the form of higher overall costs for goods and services.

The road you will travel to become debt-free may not be the most pleasant road you have traveled during your lifetime. There will be days when you will ask yourself, "Is it worth it?" Yes it is worth it, so hang in there. Best wishes to you.